PEOPLE
IN THE **NEWS**

R. L. Stine

by Joel H. Cohen

Lucent Books, San Diego, CA

Titles in the People in the News series include:

Garth Brooks

Jim Carrey

Bill Gates

John Grisham

Jesse Jackson

Michael Jordan

Stephen King

George Lucas

Dominique Moceanu

Rosie O'Donnell

Colin Powell

Christopher Reeve

The Rolling Stones

Steven Spielberg

R. L. Stine

Oprah Winfrey

Tiger Woods

Library of Congress Cataloging-in-Publication Data

Cohen, Joel H.
    R. L. Stine / by Joel H. Cohen.
        p.   cm. — (People in the news)
    Includes bibliographical references and index.
    Summary: The life of best-selling young adult horror author R. L. Stine including his childhood, the evolution of his writing career, and his popularity with both boys and girls.
    ISBN 1-56006-608-3
    1. Stine, R. L.—Juvenile literature. 2. Young adult fiction—Authorship—Juvenile literature. 3. Authors, American—20th century— Biography—Juvenile literature. 4. Horror tales—Authorship—Juvenile literature. [1. Stine, R. L. 2. Authors, American.] I. Title II. People in the news (San Diego, Calif.)
PS3569.T4837 Z63   2000
813'.54—dc21

                                                              99-050764

Table of Contents

Foreword

FAME AND CELEBRITY are alluring. People are drawn to those who walk in fame's spotlight, whether they are known for great accomplishments or for notorious deeds. The lives of the famous pique public interest and attract attention, perhaps because their experiences seem in some ways so different from, yet in other ways so similar to, our own.

Newspapers, magazines, and television regularly capitalize on this fascination with celebrity by running profiles of famous people. For example, television programs such as *Entertainment Tonight* devote all of their programming to stories about entertainment and entertainers. Magazines such as *People* fill their pages with stories of the private lives of famous people. Even newspapers, newsmagazines, and television news frequently delve into the lives of well-known personalities. Despite the number of articles and programs, few provide more than a superficial glimpse at their subjects.

Lucent's People in the News series offers young readers a deeper look into the lives of today's newsmakers, the influences that have shaped them, and the impact they have had in their fields of endeavor and on other people's lives. The subjects of the series hail from many disciplines and walks of life. They include authors, musicians, athletes, political leaders, entertainers, entrepreneurs, and others who have made a mark on modern life and who, in many cases, will continue to do so for years to come.

These biographies are more than factual chronicles. Each book emphasizes the contributions, accomplishments, or deeds that have brought fame or notoriety to the individual and shows how that person has influenced modern life. Authors portray their subjects in a realistic, unsentimental light. For example, Bill Gates—the cofounder and chief executive officer of the software giant Microsoft—has been instrumental in making personal computers the most vital tool of the modern age. Few dispute his business savvy, his perseverance, or his technical expertise, yet critics say he is ruthless in his dealings with competitors and driven more by his desire to maintain Microsoft's dominance in the computer industry than by an interest in furthering technology.

In these books, young readers will encounter inspiring stories about real people who achieved success despite enormous obstacles. Oprah Winfrey—the most powerful, most watched, and wealthiest woman on television today—spent the first six years of her life in the care of her grandparents while her unwed mother sought work and a better life elsewhere. Her adolescence was colored by promiscuity, pregnancy at age fourteen, rape, and sexual abuse.

Each author documents and supports his or her work with an array of primary and secondary source quotations taken from diaries, letters, speeches, and interviews. All quotes are footnoted to show readers exactly how and where biographers derive their information and provide guidance for further research. The quotations enliven the text by giving readers eyewitness views of the life and accomplishments of each person covered in the People in the News series.

In addition, each book in the series includes photographs, annotated bibliographies, timelines, and comprehensive indexes. For both the casual reader and the student researcher, the People in the News series offers insight into the lives of today's newsmakers—people who shape the way we live, work, and play in the modern age.

Introduction

Horribly Successful

FROM HIS IMAGINATIVE childhood on, Robert Lawrence Stine wanted to write humor, and for years he did just that, creating works that had his classmates and, later, young readers in stitches.

Then a chance came for him to write a horror novel, unexplored territory for Stine, and with publication of that book for teenagers, his literary path took a turn that would bring him success beyond his most optimistic expectations.

Still funny, "Jovial Bob," as he was known in his humor-writing days, became R. L. (for Robert Lawrence) Stine, which he felt was a more appropriate byline for a horror author. That first horror novel led to another, and another, and eventually a much-in-demand young adult horror series. So successful was the series, *Fear Street,* that he added another for younger readers. And with *Goosebumps,* his career took off like someone who has, well, seen a ghost.

By the mid-1990s, Stine was the nation's best-selling author, his two horror series outselling even the works of such celebrated writers as John Grisham and Stephen King. In fact, with 200 million copies in print, *Goosebumps* became the best-selling children's series of all time, and Stine the best-selling children's author in history.

And, incredibly, Stine (typing with one finger) produced his "safe, scary" books at the rate of *two a month!* Month after month, he produced a new book for each series, each one gobbled up by eager readers.

Stine's books gave rise to a weekly TV series and countless merchandising tie-ins. His rare book signings attracted hundreds

Horror novelist R. L. Stine, creator of the Goosebumps *and* Fear Street *series, was the nation's best-selling author in the mid-1990s.*

and hundreds of fans, and many communities throughout the country organized *Goosebumps* reading clubs.

Despite the immense popularity of Stine's books, there is some harsh criticism of their content, and a few communities have tried to keep them off library shelves. But supporters point out that Stine's books inspire children (boys especially) to read and hope that young *Goosebumps* and *Fear Street* fans will go on to read books that are more intellectually challenging and better "literature."

Who is this prolific author? What shaped him and makes him tick? Where does he get his ideas? What personal experiences does he draw on for his books? How did he come to write his hit series, and what are his writing habits? To what does he attribute his remarkable success, and how does he deal with it?

Let's find out.

Chapter 1

Just a Normal, Scary Childhood

R. L. STINE, THE best-selling children's author in history and the most successful writer of children's horror stories ever, has said that none of the scary things he writes about happened to him as a child. Yet, like all authors, what he experienced—and imagined—in his early life naturally influences what he writes as an adult.

Born on October 8, 1943, in Columbus, Ohio, Robert Lawrence Stine grew up in Bexley, a wealthy Columbus suburb. The governor's mansion was only two blocks away from the Stines' three-story brick house (which had a big yard with shade trees, built-in barbecue, and birdbath). But the Stine home was on the edge of town, three houses from the railroad tracks.

His hardworking parents were determined to make sure their children never felt poor. Bob's father, Lewis, worked for a restaurant supply company; his mother, Anne, stayed at home with the couple's three children.

Bob, the oldest (who was not known as "R. L." until he began writing horror books), recalls in his autobiography, "I felt self-conscious because my family didn't have as much money as my friends' families," and he found it hard to fit into such a wealthy town. "We couldn't afford to drive around in big cars and wear the latest, coolest clothes." But whatever feelings of exclusion he might have experienced had a plus side. "I think that my feeling like an outsider as a kid helped to make me a writer. I always seemed to be standing away from the crowd, watching everyone. I became an *observer*, which is part of what a writer does."[1]

Bob has a brother, Bill, who is three years younger, and a sister, Pam, seven years Bob's junior. The boys shared a bedroom on the second floor of the house; lying in bed and watching shadows move on the ceiling, they would take turns telling frightening stories about ghosts, haunted houses, bats, werewolves, and mummies, characters that would find their way into Bob's books years later. The stories Bob made up usually centered on a boy, who closely resembled his brother, being chased around the house by a monster.

Early Tales of Terror

A typical tale of terror would have the youngster heading for the hall closet, only to see something in it unspeakably horrible and gruesome. At that point, Bob would torture his brother by ending

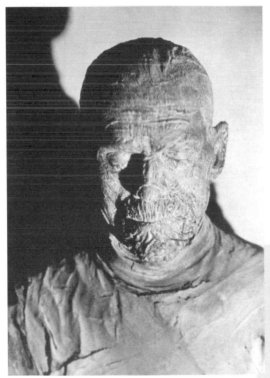

R. L. Stine's horror novels are influenced by imaginative stories about ghosts, haunted houses, bats, werewolves, and mummies that he and his brother told each other as children.

the story. "Time to go to sleep,"[2] Bob would say, ignoring his brother's pleas for him to continue. Then Bob would pretend to fall asleep with a cruel smile on his face. Now, when Stine writes a story, he tries to end each chapter with a suspenseful cliff-hanger.

"I would tell my story slowly, quietly, building the horror," he told a magazine writer. "Then when the three-headed bat was about to swoop to attack, when the mummy had his putrid, decayed hands wrapped about a throat—when I reached the very peak of suspense—I'd say, 'To be continued tomorrow. Good night.'"[3]

He admits that he was mean to his brother, and treats his readers similarly by ending each chapter with a scary image. In his autobiography, Stine speculates that he liked scary stories as a child because he found the real world rather frightening.

Above the boys' bedroom was an attic, which their mother had forbidden them to visit. Bob used to lie awake at night, wondering what terrible thing was up there. He made believe he could see through the ceiling, and he created stories about monsters, along with other things he envisioned, such as trunks and mooseheads. One day, he knew, he would venture up there.

A "Pretty Nerdy" Kid

That exploration would take considerable courage for this rather fearful youngster, neither bold nor adventurous, whose favorite pastime would be writing stories and creating magazines and comics in his room.

As to his outside activities, "I guess I was pretty nerdy," he states in his autobiography, and referring to his lack of success in sport: "I was a terribly unathletic kid."[4] When the neighborhood kids played softball on a field that extended across his backyard and two others, he was the last one chosen, and every time he batted, he grounded out to the shortstop. He couldn't shoot a basketball, and his tall, skinny body was invariably crushed in football games. He was best at bowling—that is, until he dropped the ball and broke a toe.

At day camp, Bob panicked when it was his turn to qualify for his Red Cross Turtle badge. Qualifying required jumping in the pool and swimming to the other side and back. With the other campers and counselors watching and urging him to jump, he just walked away. Whenever Stine writes about a kid who is really terrified, he recalls how he felt then and tries to incorporate that fear and anxiety into his character.

Stine, who to this day has to climb rather than jump into a swimming pool, says, "It's important for a horror writer to know *true* horror."[5]

Often, he will try to recall the things that frightened him when he was a child: the dark, for instance, or the fear that someone was waiting behind the garage or hiding in the closet.

But "he wasn't afraid of spiders, ghosts or alligators under the bed, the typical terrors of childhood,"[6] writes Holly Pupino in the *Ohio State Alumni Magazine*. "No, I was totally afraid of everything," Stine told Pupino. "It was like a paranoia. I would worry about walking into the dining room and having the light fall on my head."[7]

Never Bitten by a Vampire

While he would later make use of his various childhood fears in his books, Stine never actually experienced the bizarre events that frighten his characters. He told newspaperman Ross Raihala:

> One of the questions I'm asked most often is "Did any of the things in your scary novels ever happen to you in real life?" Kids are always disappointed, but I have to tell them no. I've never been terrorized by a maniac, haunted by a ghost from the future, frozen alive inside a snowman, been bitten by a vampire or come back from the dead. I got a very bad paper cut once. But that's about the most horrifying thing that's ever happened to me.[8]

A painful event of a different sort occurred when Bob was seven. The family had to move because his father had changed jobs and the family could no longer afford the house in which they'd been living. When Bob got the news of the impending move, he decided that if he and his kid brother were ever going to discover the secret of the attic, they had to act right away.

Bill feared their mother would be furious if she found out that Bobby, as Bob was then called, was going to explore the forbidden place. But Bob warned him that if he dared tell their mother, the dreaded Captain Grashus would "get" him. The captain was an invincible superhero Bob had dreamed up and could become (with a bath-towel "cape" tied around his neck); Bill was the Grashus Ranger, whose mission was to do exactly what the Captain told him to do, such as cutting the grass or cleaning their room.

When it came to the fearsome attic, though, the Ranger wasn't obeying orders, and Bob had to explore the attic himself. So up he went into the dark, cobwebby mystery place, finding neither trunks nor mooseheads nor monsters. What he saw were his mother's old dresses and his father's old workpants and a small, dust-covered black case, which turned out to contain a portable typewriter. When he poked at the keys with his index finger, they worked.

Turning back, Bob was startled to see his mother, who reminded him that she had warned the boys about the attic, which, with its rotting floors, wasn't safe. But she let him keep the typewriter, and he used it to write his own short stories, entire magazines, and comics, which he also illustrated.

According to Stine, his parents didn't know what to make of his writing. "I just wanted to write. I don't really know why. I just always loved it more than anything else." His parents "kept telling me to go outside and play. But I ignored them, and just kept typing away."[9]

He was nine years when he started making up joke books on that old typewriter. The books, he told writer Vivian Rose, "were terrible, but I loved doing it." Bob also illustrated the joke books and recalls that his ambition was to draw comics like those from EC Horror Comics: "I really wanted to be a cartoonist, but I couldn't draw. So I became a writer."[10]

Once a Duck, Always a Duck

For Stine, who claims to love all scary things, Halloween was a favorite holiday: "When I was a kid, I had one costume. It was a duck outfit, and I would wear it on Halloween every year. My entire childhood was spent in a duck costume. I was so embarrassed,"[11] he told *USA Today.* Stine incorporated the duck costume in his book, *The Haunted Mask.*

Among other youthful traumas that served as raw material for Stine's creativity was the experience of baby-sitting, along with Bill, young cousins who turned into "monsters" once their parents went out. Those challenging sessions gave him the idea for another of his books, *The Baby-Sitter.*

As a youngster, the scary things Stine loved originated from a variety of sources. "One of my earliest memories is this voice [that of the announcer for the popular series, *Suspense*] coming

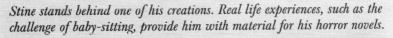

Stine stands behind one of his creations. Real life experiences, such as the challenge of baby-sitting, provide him with material for his horror novels.

out of the radio: 'Tales calcu-
lated to keep you in suspense.'
I turned it right off," [12] he told
writer James Kaplan, who adds
that Stine turned it right back
on again, as soon as he found
his courage.

At a young age, Stine en-
joyed reading science fiction,
especially works by Isaac
Asimov and Ray Bradbury.
The latter's *Something Wicked
This Way Comes* is Bob's favorite "scary" book. Dealing
with the dark side of human
nature, it tells of the involve-
ment of two thirteen-year-old
boys with a mysterious carnival
that comes to town and a mysterious ringmaster, Mr. Dark,

As a child, Stine fervently read the works of science-fiction writer Isaac Asimov (pictured).

who grants wishes with terrifying consequences. Another of
Stine's favorite science fiction authors is Robert Sheckley, whose
Mindswap remains lodged in his memory. The book is about a
company that will place a human's mind in the body of an alien
on another planet, and the alien's mind into the human's body,
for two weeks.

Even scenes from *Pinocchio*—the original book, not the Disney
movie—made an impression that translated into his later writings.
Stine's mother had read the book aloud to him when he was a
child, and he always remembered Pinocchio smashing his cricket
conscience against the wall and having his own feet burnt off when
he fell asleep with them on the stove. *Pinocchio* partly inspired
Stine's idea of a puppet coming to life in more than one of his horror novels.

When Bob was old enough to read by himself, he eagerly de-
voured everything from fairy tales to Greek myths and Norse leg-
ends. He had no interest in reading about real people or events.

Bob read all Edgar Allan Poe's stories at a young age, and every week after Sunday school would go with his brother to watch such 1950s horror movies as *It Came from Beneath the Sea*, *Night of the Living Dead*, and *The Creature from the Black Lagoon*. The boys especially enjoyed movies in which a monster would level a major city, at which they'd scream and kick the seats in front of them. When trying to come up with a good book title, Stine sometimes recalls the scary movies he and his brother were so fond of.

Although he was fascinated by spooky stories as a child, it never occurred to Bob to try writing children's horror fiction because his main interest was in being funny. His life's ambition was to have his own humor magazine.

Hair-Raising Tales at the Barbershop

As his fondness for reading humor—and horror—magazines developed, Bob discovered an unusual "library." While awaiting his turn in a barbershop, he picked up his first *Mad* magazine,

The beast from Revenge of the Creature *haunts the depths. Stine and his brother were enraptured by movies such as* The Creature from the Black Lagoon.

originally published as an EC comic before it became a full-size magazine. His parents thought the magazine (which he found hilarious) was trash and would not allow it in the house. So Bob went for a haircut just about every Saturday, to be sure of not missing an issue. And at the same "library," he discovered the gruesome, blood-and-guts comic books *Tales from the Crypt* and *The Vault of Horror*. To keep up with the latest gross installments, virtually every week he would ask his mother for a dollar for the barbershop: "I had no hair at all when I was a kid,"[13] the balding author jokes.

Asked to name his childhood heroes, he says he admired many writers and funny people, among them contributors to EC Horror Comics and *Mad* magazine.

In the Stines' second house, the brothers took turns terrifying each other with made-up horror tales. A sure-fire chill-inducer was the story of a man who, they decided, had been murdered in the bedroom in which they now slept. According to their story, the victim was buried under a pile of smooth, white

Stine habitually went to a barbershop like this one so that he could keep up with his favorite magazines.

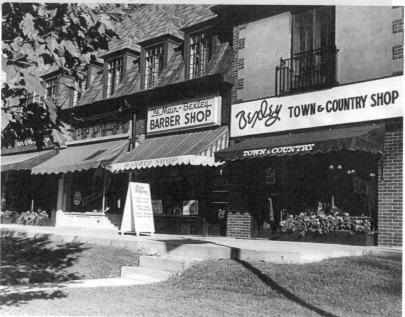

rocks that stood in the middle of the woods behind the fence at the edge of their backyard. After the mound of white stones disappeared, the brothers never spoke of it again, but sometimes, when he starts writing a book, Bob thinks about the mound and the goosebumps it inspired.

Scariest Memory

R. L. Stine's scariest Halloween memory, he told *USA Today* in a Halloween 1996 interview, is of a backyard exploration at his suburban Columbus, Ohio, home when Bob was ten and his brother Bill was seven.

[The house had] a long strip of a back yard, and behind it there was a stretch of woods. In the woods, there was a mound made of smooth white stones. We had no idea what it was, but it was round and high enough for kids to climb on.

Everyone in the neighborhood would hang out there; it was like a secret hiding place. We'd all climb on the stones, sit on this pile and wonder what was underneath. . . .

We knew never to go there at night. That's because we all believed that someone was buried under this pile of stones.

One Halloween—it was late and we had done our trick-or-treating —we had gone to bed. And then I remember saying to my brother, "You know, it's Halloween; we should go back there and find out what this pile really is. If anyone should go, we should." So we could brag about it later.

We waited for our parents to go to sleep, then got dressed and got our flashlights. We crept out of the house, across the back yard and stepped into the woods.

Well, we got about halfway to the pile and we heard this clank, clank, clunk. It was like the sound of stones hitting stones.

Something was back there. Clunk, clunk. Clunk.

And that's when we turned back to the house—and ran. We never made it to the mound. And we never talked about it, never told anyone we had even tried. It was so terrifying.

I think about this now—it was a really scary moment of my childhood. When I sit down to write, I am always reminded— and amazed—that something as simple as a pile of stones could hold such horror.

What we saw in our imaginations was worse than anything out there—it was very ordinary but very, very scary.

Because the Stine family did not own a television set until Bob was nine, he spent a lot of time listening to the radio, enjoying nightly mystery shows, comedies, and westerns, among them *The Lone Ranger, The Shadow, Gang Busters,* and, of course, *Suspense,* the program whose chilling opening announcement used to scare him so much. Stine tries to make his books as scary as the *Suspense* announcer's terrifying voice.

In later years, Bob came to love the humor of radio personality Jean Shepherd, who, in live broadcasts from New York City from midnight to 5 A.M., told intriguing, funny stories about his childhood, family, friends, and the city. Shepherd inspired in Stine a love of storytelling and a desire to live in New York. Eventually, he would move to the big city and tell stories.

Back in Ohio, Bob was not even in his teens when he launched his magazine-writing "career" with *THE ALL NEW BOB STINE GIGGLE BOOK,* a miniature ten-page production with five pages of corny jokes and riddles. His next effort, in 1956, was *HAH, for Maniacs Only!,* which spoofed popular TV shows of the day, such as *The 64-Thousand-Dollar Question* (which in Stine's version became *The 64-Thousand-Dollar Answer*) and *Dragnet* (which he renamed *Dragnut*). This was followed by such attention-grabbers as *Tales to Drive You Batty* and *Whammy,* in which he credited himself with every title from editor to contributing artist to janitor. Then came *Bozos on Patrol, Stine's Line,* and *BARF,* in which he attached funny captions to pictures he cut from magazines.

He spent many hours on these publications, creating characters, making up jokes, and doing all the jobs necessary to produce a magazine. And when his parents asked him what he wanted as a gift for his bar mitzvah (when, at the age of thirteen, Jewish boys become religiously responsible for their actions), Bob did not hesitate a moment. Hooked on writing, he asked for a new typewriter. His parents complied, presenting him with a heavy-duty machine that he used for years.

Author Stine was on his way.

Chapter 2

Eloquent Insanity

S TINE'S JUNIOR HIGH school classmates were treated to more of his original writing efforts, which featured corny jokes and made-up characters, beginning with Sooper Stooge. In *FEEF*, for example, Stine's invented character Harvey Poobah fell off the Empire State Building and lived (until he hit the ground).

The budding writer was delighted to watch his friends reading his "masterpieces," especially when a teacher caught someone reading a Stine production instead of the class's assignment. A memorable incident involved Bob's *From Here to Insanity*, which lasted seven issues, and, among other things, spoofed well-known characters such as Robin Hood, whom he dubbed "Robin Hoodlum." A student was enjoying one *Insanity* issue during class, laughing out loud at Bob's jokes. But the teacher was not amused at the outburst and confiscated the copy. The teacher then proceeded to read aloud an excerpt from one of the articles, titled "How to Read This Magazine in Class." One piece of expert advice in the article: "If the teacher asks what you're reading, say it is a pocket dictionary!" Bob and the rest of the class roared with laughter, but the teacher, dealing freedom of the press a blow, marched Bob down to the principal's office.

However disruptive-though-funny Bob might have been, there was little that school authorities could do with him, since despite his greater interest in writing than in schoolwork, he always got A's and B's.

In high school, Bob continued to write funny material and to produce his own magazines, under such provocative titles as *Eloquent Insanity* and *Uproarious Utopia*. His school writing assignments also brought him acclaim, and, in the case of several essays, prizes. He was the natural choice to write the senior class skit, a creation he titled "TV Programs That Have Distracted Us and Kept Us from Studying While We Were in High School." When the skit was performed, Stine was thrilled to see the audience laughing at *his* words. Students may also have laughed at a slogan he created for a friend's campaign for president of the senior class, "Kick the Scoundrel In." Despite the witty slogan, his friend lost the election in a landslide.

Stine had musical, as well as writing, talent, but like many people who find it difficult to do two things at once, Bob realized he was unable to play clarinet *and* march in the school band simultaneously. So he decided to give up the band in favor of the school chorus, which did not march.

Outside school, he and a friend created and tape-recorded comedy routines complete with made-up characters. His creative writing extended to other fields, as well. Bob tried his hand at writing a novel, an effort he considered worthwhile if only be-

R. L. Stine's (back row, left) creativity and humor were greeted warmly by his high-school classmates.

Singing in the high-school choir was one of the many activities in which the multitalented Stine (back row, center) participated.

cause it got him out of doing chores like working in the yard. Years later, recalling his unsuccessful attempt to write a serious grown-up novel, he told a reporter: "I never really had anything to say. I never had this burning desire to write some heavy thing. I've always been a genre writer. I love the stuff." [14]

Beyond the written word, he was fascinated with the moving image. The visual adaptations of Rod Serling's stories in the 1960s TV series *Twilight Zone* influenced Stine's later writing.

Campus Comedy

In his senior year, real-life choices loomed large, especially college. His first choice was Ohio State University, and his acceptance for admission to that institution in 1961 made him very happy for several reasons. Because the Columbus-based university was just a bus ride away from his house, he could live at home, which certainly was cheaper than a dorm, and continue to enjoy his mother's delicious cooking. But what electrified Bob about the acceptance was the opportunity to write for *Sundial,* the college's well-known humor magazine. It was something he had dreamed about, even in high school.

Stine was attracted to Ohio State (pictured) because of the opportunity to write for its well-known magazine, Sundial.

The magazine had some celebrated alumni. Milt Caniff, creator of the comic strip, *Steve Canyon*, contributed artwork to *Sundial* when he was at Ohio State in the 1930s. World-famous humorist James Thurber, who became a writer and cartoonist for the *New Yorker*, was once a *Sundial* writer (and Bob was thrilled to follow in his footsteps).

While writing for the magazine was a dream come true, Bob had an even bigger ambition: he wanted to be the publication's editor. By the end of his freshman year, he applied for the job to the Publications Board, most of whose members were professors and, in Bob's words, "very cautious people, [who] wanted to judge how much of a troublemaker I might be. I tried to look harmless." [15] Aided by samples of his work, Bob convinced the board he could do the job and was appointed editor, a position he held for three years. He gave himself the name Jovial Bob, hoping to make this personage a running character in the magazine.

Aiming to provide plenty of laughs, Stine and *Sundial,* with typical college humor, ridiculed virtually all aspects of campus life, from dorms to dating. Favorite targets were the men's and women's deans and the rules they enforced, such as curfews: in those days, many colleges required female undergraduates to be back in their dorms as early as 8 P.M.; there was no such rule for male students. Among features of the twenty-five-cent magazine were cartoons, phony ads, and a feature that would come in handy in his early professional career, fake interviews.

The student newspaper, the *Lantern,* liked to take jabs at *Sundial,* and, in response, Bob reports in his autobiography, he enlisted letter writers to take his side. One called him "a man of infinite wit and talent" and went on to say, "I would have made these same statements even if my brother hadn't forced me." [16]

In 1964, *Makio,* the Ohio State yearbook, joked, "As the year went on, he [Jovial Bob] became less jovial." Then, under the heading, "Sundial Provides Parodies, Satire," the yearbook reported:

Writing for Sundial, *Stine and the rest of the magazine's staff satirized virtually every aspect of campus life.*

"Sundial hit the campus this year with six big issues, and the campus hardly had a chance to hit back. The humor magazine, now in its 53rd year, offered OSU students what it called 'a look at the world through prose-colored glasses.'"

Not only its prose but a pose (a photo feature) contributed to the magazine's popularity. The bulk of *Sundial*'s readership was male, so every issue carried photos of a good-looking "Girl of the Month." The young women selected for the "honor" were Ohio State students, but in one issue, the magazine printed a photo of a movie starlet instead, and gave her the made-up name of Pamela Winters. Compounding the hoax, *Sundial* gave the number of the university's Student Senate office as the nonexistent Ms. Winter's number.

The starlet's picture led to record-breaking sales (eight thousand copies in one day!) and, no surprise, the Senate's phone rang constantly with calls from male students seeking "Pamela." But the student senators got their revenge. One, pretending to be "Pamela Winters," invited callers to "stop by sometime" and gave them Stine's home address and phone number. Years later, he used that basic idea in a *Goosebumps* volume titled *Calling All Creeps!* In it, the same kind of prank backfires, as the practical

A Buckeye Bull's-Eye: Laughter and Libel

The 1963 edition of the Ohio State University yearbook, *Makio*, credited *Sundial* with bringing "Humor to Buckeye Campus," and carried this "glowing" review of the magazine:

> Among other disasters, this year Ohio State received seven attacks of *SUNDIAL*, the neoteric [modern] world of laughter, presenting a barrage of bluster to burn the bearers of bursting bravado and blast the backdrops off bullet-headed bureaucrats.

> Featuring an expanded format, editor Robert Lawrence Stine, managing editor Penny I. Wainer, feature editor Joseph Arthur, and art editor Carol Nicklaus led the crafty, crazy crusade against hypocrisy, pomposity, and absurdity.

> Continually taking light jabs at the campus community, *SUNDIAL* came up with parodies of the Columbus "Dispatch," the "Lantern," . . . "True Confessions" magazine, the Greek [campus fraternity] system, and the administration. *SUNDIAL* combined laughter and libel in a potpourri of paranoia and piercing polemics.

SUNDIAL

The Zoo Around Us   25¢

ALL NEW SICKENING FORMAT!
Appalling Conclusion:
THE LAST ANGRY WEREWOLF
PORNOGRAPHY IN THE LANTERN!
Special:
MEET THE EXCITING SINGING
GROUP FROM ENGLAND!

The playful Sundial *was full of pranks that Stine later turned into ideas for his horror novels.*

joker gets calls from creepy creatures with scaly purple skin and sharp fangs.

Promising "Absolutely Nothing"

Jovial Bob's practical joking was not limited to the pages of *Sundial*. One memorable extended prank was his campaign for the presidency of the Student Senate during his senior year in college. The university had a rule stating that a candidate had to be a junior, but Bob had a ready rationale for his candidacy. "During the past year," he told the student newspaper, "the students of Ohio State have come to expect absolutely nothing from the senate. Since I'm graduating this spring and won't be around next year, I feel I'm in a better position than the other candidates to give the students absolutely nothing." He ran newspaper ads declaring that "as a public service," Jovial Bob would not appear at this or that campus location. Stine

The Power and Magic of Writing: Seeing Evil Through Innocent Eyes

Bob was nineteen when he read the first book that "actually scared" him. The novel by Ray Bradbury called *Something Wicked This Way Comes* "had me terrified," and to this day, he declared in a Book Country advertisement in the *New York Times,* on September 23, 1998, it "remains the scariest book I have ever read."

He also learned important lessons from the book, in which two boys sneak out of their homes late at night to watch a "mysterious carnival set up its tents, and are drawn into nightmare after nightmare of pure evil."

"Thanks to Ray Bradbury, I learned something about the power of seeing evil through innocent eyes and I discovered something about the power and magic of writing."

Ray Bradbury.

campaigned on the slogan "Elect a clown for President," and several staff members, dressed in clown costumes, would tell prospective voters that "all of the candidates were clowns—but only Jovial Bob was clown enough to admit it." [17] The university refused to put the ineligible candidate's name on the ballot, but Jovial Bob fared pretty well: though he lost the election, he received 1,163 write-in votes of the 8,727 votes cast.

The 1965 edition of the Ohio State yearbook printed two photos of *Sundial* staffers. One showed the staff gathered around a student stretched out on a table. "'Sundial has created a Monster!' cries Jovial Bob." The caption under the other photo read: "'I always enjoy encouraging new writers,' says Jovial Bob. Here he encourages one by smiling at him as he rips his story in half."

Actually, he enjoyed good relationships with fellow magazine staffers. (One, Joe Arthur, would collaborate on Stine's autobiography.) Under Stine's wacky guidance, *Sundial* flourished. A headline in the 1965 edition of the university yearbook proclaimed: "*Sundial*, 'World's Funniest College Magazine,'" a reference to its position as number-one on-campus magazine in the

In 1965 Sundial *was the number-one on-campus magazine in the United States.*

MARCH   PRICE: TWENTY-FIVE CENTS

SUNDIAL

WORLD'S FUNNIEST COLLEGE MAGAZINE

United States that year according to the annual poll of college magazine editors.

"Under the leadership of Editor 'Jovial' Bob Stine," the yearbook reported, "the *Sundial* staff produced a new-sized magazine that hit a record high for circulation in *Sundial*'s 53-year history. Much of this success can be attributed to the Sundial Girl-of-the-Month telephone number hoax, the Dating and Morality issue, the Big Farm sweatshirts, 'Jovial' Bob's presidential campaign, and a mixture of humorous and satirical prose."

Carefree college days could not continue indefinitely, of course. And when the English-studying, fun-loving prankster earned his bachelor's degree from Ohio State in June 1965, it was time for Stine to face life. He would do it in characteristically inimitable fashion.

Chapter 3

Bologna Sandwiches, Soda Caps, and Bananas

Bob HAD DREAMED of pursuing a writing career in New York City, but settling there, he knew, would take a lot of money, certainly more than the savings he had in the bank. So he looked for work near home, and found it: a job as a substitute teacher.

Within a few months, English major Stine was hired to teach history full time. Suspecting that many of his pupils were like himself in not being particularly interested in history, Bob did what he could to motivate them, and even offered an incentive: if they behaved themselves Monday through Thursday, Friday would be "free reading day." And the "free" part was no exaggeration. They could read anything they wanted, including comic books. In his autobiography, he writes: "I emphasized the comic books because I loved comic books and I thought maybe some of my students did too. Besides, they might have a few titles I hadn't read."

So for several Fridays, Stine and his students shared comic books, sometimes reading them aloud. Bob happened to be reading *Spider-Man* when the "super-strict" principal came in to observe him. Stine expected an outburst, but the principal merely looked at the students, then at him, scowled and stormed out. He never mentioned the occurrence to Stine.

"I don't know if my students learned anything, but I sure did," Stine writes in his autobiography. "Teaching gave me time to watch kids in action. I was able to listen to what they said and the way they said it. I think my characters' conversations in *Fear Street* and *Goosebumps* are more true to life because of my real-life year in the classroom." [18] Later, when starting a new book, he sometimes pictured his students and thought about their actions and feelings.

When not teaching, Stine worked on a two-minute comedy radio program about Captain Anything, a superhero with horn-rimmed eyeglasses (the type Stine then wore) who could transform himself into anything, although his glasses remained unchanged. Bob wrote the scripts and, working late at night in a recording studio, had two popular Columbus radio personalities provide the voices. He hoped to sell Captain Anything scripts to radio stations throughout the country, but after receiving four sample episodes, stations were *anything* but interested.

There was, however, a pleasant realization for Bob as the school year ended. He decided he had enough money saved to pay for a month's rent in New York, and in the fall of 1966 he headed for the big city.

Interviews Made (Up) to Order

In New York's Greenwich Village, Stine was delighted and over-whelmed by what he found—bookstores that stayed open all night, specialty stores devoted exclusively to such merchandise as lightbulbs or windup toys or rubber chickens. But the serious business of finding a place to live and a job took priority, so he rented a tiny one-room apartment, and, while looking for work, subsisted on bologna sandwiches.

While Bob's dream was to get a writing job on a major magazine, he realized that at that stage of his career, it was a goal beyond his reach. So he tried elsewhere. He applied for a job with a magazine called *Institutional Investor*, despite having no understanding of the stock market. At the job interview, Bob pretended to be familiar with the magazine although he had never seen an issue. However, the job for which he was apply-ing turned out to involve production work rather than writing. Confident that he could learn the necessary production skills,

Although Stine was impressed with New York's Greenwich Village, he quickly discovered the difficulty of finding work there.

Bob accepted the job but was fired almost immediately when the art director found that he had no idea of how to put in "running feet" (the magazine's name, issue date, and page number at the bottom of each page).

Stine's job search took him next not to an office but an apartment on New York's Upper West Side. There, he was greeted by a middle-aged woman (who, according to one account, never left her apartment or her brown bathrobe). She told Bob she edited six teenage fan magazines, which competed with the best-selling mass-marketed titles, even approximating their names. For example, *15* competed with the hottest teen magazine of the moment, *16*.

As Stine recounts in *It Came from Ohio!* the editor hardly looked at his work samples before giving him an assignment: write an interview with Glen Campbell. When Stine asked for the country music star's telephone number, the editor replied: "I didn't say *do* an interview. I said write an interview."

"You mean make it up?"

"You got it." [19]

She handed Bob several newspaper clippings and a few photographs of the singer, explaining that he should use information from the newspaper articles to develop a story to accompany the photos. Stine wrote the article—a fictional piece titled "Glen Campbell: Two Men I Call Friend"—in less than an hour, and it appeared in *Country & Western Music*. He went on to write "interview" stories of such other big stars as the Beatles, Tom Jones, the Rolling Stones, and the Jackson Five, the group that launched Michael Jackson, without ever actually interviewing them.

Ghostly Tales

Realizing he had to be fast and creative, Stine creatively had lead singer Diana Ross leaving the Supremes in one magazine and staying with the hot Motown vocal group in another. When he asked if the subjects of the fictional articles ever sued the magazine, the editor said no, they wanted all the publicity they could get.

Stine's career as a legitimate fiction writer got a boost when the editor's boss launched a horror magazine, *Adventures in Horror*. Beginning with "Bony Fingers from the Grave," his first published horror fiction piece, Bob, using the byline Robert Lawrence, contributed a host of ghostly tales to the publication, while continuing to create dozens of celebrity interview stories for the other magazines. The weekly hundred-dollar salary enabled Bob to skip the bologna (at least the sandwiches) and treat himself to an occasional meal in a restaurant. But after barely a month, the magazine enterprise went out of business, and Bob was unemployed again.

Not for long, however. He soon landed a writing job at a magazine called *Soft Drink Industry*, for which he wrote articles about sodas, soda cans, syrups, and the people who made them. His articles were probably of considerable interest to the soft drink industry but not to him.

Hoping to land another job, Bob kept searching the want ads. And, one lunch hour late in 1968, he found one. When he broke the news to his boss that he was leaving, the editor could not believe Bob's decision to abandon the world of bottle caps.

Bob Goes Bananas

Stine's new job was with Scholastic, Inc., a well-known publisher of books and magazines for young readers. Hired originally as a staff writer of news and history articles for *Junior Scholastic* magazine, he went on to become editor of the company's social studies publication, *Scholastic Search*, and others, including *Wheels*, a magazine for teenagers taking driver education classes. For one article, he had a writer canvas police stations throughout the country for the wildest alibis heard from traffic violators.

Stine enjoyed the fast pace of working on a weekly magazine: planning, writing, editing, or proofreading four different

Signs of the Times

The first time Bob Stine appeared at a store to autograph copies of a book he had written (*How to Be Funny*, published by E. P. Dutton in 1978), he was wearing bunny ears.

The reason? "Jovial Bob" felt that to promote a funny book he should wear something funny. And, in joking about a possible title for a sequel to *How to Be Funny*, he had suggested *How to Be Bunny*. So, ready to autograph copies of his silly guidebook at the Doubleday bookstore on Fifth Avenue in New York City, he was outfitted with rabbit ears.

A rabbit's *foot* for luck might have been a better idea, since he sold and signed a grand total of one book!

But it was an entirely different story at Stine book signings years later, when the *Goosebumps* series was a runaway hit. At one such event, at a mall near Washington, D.C., the author was swamped by an estimated five thousand youngsters, seven times the number expected.

In fact, the crowd had become dangerously big. So, reluctantly, Stine sent four thousand of the autograph seekers home. Shouting into a microphone, he explained to the disappointed throng that it would have taken him eight hours to get to them.

The author, who made very few personal appearances after that, shared his feelings about book-signing sessions with writer Kim Haub: "It sounds weird but too many kids come. Any time you have to send 4,000 kids home, it is not a good day."

issues at once. "Magazine writing was the perfect training for me. I learned to write fast—and move on to the next piece," Stine declares in his autobiography. "I'm a very lucky writer. I've always been able to write quickly, and it usually comes out the way I want it on the first try."[20]

An opportunity to produce an entire magazine just the way he wanted it came in the early 1970s. Scholastic appointed Stine to produce and edit a wacky, weekly humor magazine, *Bananas*, which he envisioned as being in the spirit of *Mad* magazine, and for which Bob himself wrote most of the articles. An opportunity like this was, for Stine, a lifetime fantasy realized: "My ambition in life was to have my own humor magazine, and I actually achieved it when I was 28. I had the magazine *Bananas* for ten years. And that was really fun. I always loved writing humor."[21]

The *Bananas* type of humor took the form of such continuing characters as Phil Fly and ads promoting such products as water with 50 percent fewer calories. The magazine also featured off-the-wall articles, illustrated by equally zany artwork. Titles included "How to Turn Your Uncle into a Coffee Table" and "20 Things You Can Do with a Rubber Chicken."

One thing Stine actually did with a rubber chicken was hang it in his office, claiming it was a first at the company, a claim few could or would challenge. He also contends he was the first [male] editor not to wear a tie to work. One of his favorite extracurricular fun activities was sending fellow employees fake but official-looking memos. Some examples: having everyone move down one office to the right, to alleviate an office space problem, and alerting everyone to come to work in a raincoat and to cover their papers because of a scheduled all-day test of the overhead sprinkler system. The memos were phony, of course, but to Bob's delight some took them seriously.

What Jovial (but shy) Bob had taken quite seriously—gone "bananas" over, you might say, before he founded the magazine of the same name—was Jane Waldhorn, a young woman just out of college, whom he had met at a friend's party in the late 1960s. Jane would become his wife on June 22, 1969, the mother of their only child, Matthew Daniel, on June 7, 1980, and, years later, Bob's editor.

Jane also came to work for Scholastic, first writing (authentic) celebrity interviews for *Scholastic Scope* magazine, and then, shortly before Bob launched *Bananas*, becoming editor of *Dynamite*, the country's most popular kids' magazine.

Bananas, too, was a huge success, its appeal extending beyond its young readership to the book publishing world. "One day," Bob recalls, "an editor [Ellen Rudin] at Dutton called and said, 'I love your magazine; I bet you could write funny kids' books.' So I said, 'OK.' She gave me a contract. I never go looking for contracts, people just give me these things." What emerged in 1978 was Stine's first published children's book, *How to Be Funny,* which, according to its author, was "a very subversive book. It tells you how to get a big laugh at the dinner table, how to be funny during study hall. Parents hated that book."[22]

Bananas Splits

While many people loved *Bananas*, none more than Stine, the uninhibited fun would not last forever, and, in 1984, after a decade of publication, the magazine folded. Stine had been hearing word that he was about to be out of a job and, although he was never actually called in by his boss, the rumor was true. Stine was devastated: "They had to fire me four times," he told newsman Murray Dubin. "I couldn't believe they wanted me to go home."[23]

Although Stine no longer regards being fired as the end of the world, and even goes so far as to recommend the experience, it was a shocking blow in 1984. To make ends meet while looking for other work, he "went home and wrote all kinds of things. . . . [For example] at the bottom of every page of a coloring book there is a line telling a little story. Thirty-two pages and 32 lines of copy, $500 a book."[24] He was able to do captions for two or three coloring books a day, among them Bullwinkle and Mighty Mouse, work he mightily enjoyed.

He also wrote joke books with such titles as *101 Silly Monster Jokes, Sick of Being Sick,* and *Bored of Being Bored,* GI Joe action stories, Indiana Jones novels, junior James Bond books, multiple-ending mystery books for kids, *Madballs* (a series of books about rubber balls with faces), and even bubble gum cards. "Somebody's got to write that stuff," he remarks. "When you start out as a freelancer, you don't say no to anybody."[25]

True to his philosophy, Stine did not say no when the producer of Nickelodeon's *Eureeka's Castle*, a TV program for preschool children featuring puppets, invited him to be its head writer. Stine quickly found that TV writing was a group project; in addition to staff writers, producers, directors, and performers had a say in the final script, a working arrangement that resulted in numerous revisions. Stine and his staff of writers produced a hundred hours of scripts, as well as four half-hour specials. After its first year, the program won an Ace Award, cable TV's top honor, as best children's show.

A Most Memorable "Blind Date"

In 1986 Stine kept a lunch date with a friend, Jean Feiwel, then editorial director and associate publisher at Scholastic. Little did he know that he was headed for a "blind date" with publishing history. When Feiwel suggested that he could write a great horror novel for teenage readers, Stine claims not to have known what she was talking about. But he readily agreed. The publishing executive told him merely to go home and write a book called *Blind Date*.

Never having read the type of book the publisher wanted, Stine started researching novels of that genre and tried to figure out what he could do that was different. He determined to make his book cleaner and funnier than the others. In addition, as he told Fred Kaplan, he decided "to go for a younger audience," because he had "written humor books for 8- to 12-year-olds," adding: "That's my mental level, I think."[26]

Stine took three months to write the horror book from nothing more than its title, a very leisurely pace compared to his current production: "Three months! What a luxury that would be now."[27]

Blind Date, "horrible" as Stine intended it to be, tells of a boy who keeps getting calls from a girl claiming to be his blind date although she has been dead for three years. Incorporating sug-

It's going to be a real scream....

Blind Date *(cover shown here),
Stine's first book in the horror
genre, became a best-seller in
1986.*

gestions from his wife, Stine, who hates making revisions, spent
a month revising the manuscript of the book, which Scholastic,
the company that had fired him, published in 1986.

To Stine's complete and pleasant surprise, *Blind Date* was an
immediate best-seller, even among boys, with more than half a
million copies sold. He had struck a chord with young readers,
who obviously liked books that were scary.

Successful, too, was his next book, which Scholastic had
asked him to write a year later. *Twisted* is about a sorority whose
deranged members commit a murder every year. A third scary
novel by Stine, *The Baby-Sitter*, was also a best-seller. Despite the
success of those early titles, he did not think he could make a living doing one book a year.

Then how about a series? The thought came to Stine as he
pored over mail from readers requesting more frightening novels.
He discussed the prospect with his wife and Joan Waricha, both of
whom had left positions at Scholastic in 1983 to form their own

company, Parachute Press, which would become a leading independent producer of books for children. They liked the idea of having Bob write a series of horror novels for nine- to fourteen-year-olds. But the series needed a memorable general title, and when the name *Fear Street* popped into Bob's head, he knew it was right for what would be the first young adult horror series.

Stine, encouraged by the success of his books, began to publish his horror novels in series.

The partners brought the *Fear Street* idea to Pocket Books, a major publisher, which commissioned three novels for the series and then three more. The first, *The New Girl,* was published in 1989, followed by *The Surprise Party* and *The Overnight.* With Stine producing the best-sellers at the rate of one a month, his career as *horrormeister* was well under way.

"Jekyll and Hyde"

Writing horror books was a major transition for Stine, who had written "funny" for children for twenty-six years, and had never intended to be scary. But he was readily adapting to the new genre. "Someone once called me the 'Jekyll and Hyde of children's books,'" he says, "and I guess that's about right. I wrote about 30 or 40 joke books and humor books before I slipped into my 'horror' identity. These days, I'm scary all the time."[28] Still, he incorporates humor into his horror novels, and, in any case, he enjoys writing books of both kinds.

Switching from funny to scary also brought about a name change. While he was writing funny books, he was called Jovial Bob Stine, but he switched to R. L. Stine now, because he considered this name to be scarier than Jovial Bob.

"R. L." was doing fine with *Fear Street* when Joan Waricha suggested an additional book series for him to try: scary books for younger children that would be scary and funny—full of thrills and chills but minus the gore. Pleased with the idea, Stine set out to find a series title. He discovered it in a television station's ad in *TV Guide* promoting "Goosebumps week." *Goosebumps* is what his new series became.

Geared to children ages eight to twelve, *Goosebumps* made its debut in July 1992 with *Welcome to Dead House* which became an instant hit, selling millions of copies. Recalling that first effort, Stine says, "I really didn't have it down yet. [*Dead House* is] much scarier than the others. So the rest are toned down, with more humor. I decided I didn't want to have dead kids in my books."[29] The difference between the series, as he sees it, is that nobody dies in *Goosebumps* while many teens perish in *Fear Street*.

Stine was soon turning out books for both series in rapid-fire order, books that many hundreds of thousands of young readers would eagerly devour. By 1994, *Goosebumps* books were being shipped to bookstores at the rate of 1.25 million a month! As Stine would later tell young readers, he found it very exciting to go into a bookstore and see so many shelves filled with his works.

How Stine manages to produce this steady stream of best-sellers is astonishing: his method is to use the classic combination of inspiration and perspiration, but with major differences.

Chapter 4

R. L.'s M.O.—The Method to Stine's Madness

WHILE MOST AUTHORS take many months, even years, to write a book, Stine produces them at the remarkable rate of two every month. He completes twenty-four books a year—more in six months than most authors do in six years.

Pounding away at a typewriter (he's since switched to a computer) with what one writer described as a single, "crooked and gnarled"[30] finger, Stine takes about three days to outline and eight days to write a *Goosebumps*—each book averaging 125 printed pages—and about ten to twelve days to write a *Fear Street*, a pace the author acknowledges to be inhuman. In the words of one newspaperman, Stine works on deadlines, "that would make the toughest newspaper reporter cringe."[31]

"I'm a machine," says Stine, who turns out twenty manuscript pages a day for six and occasionally seven days a week. He further declares, "I'm lucky. Kids ask me all the time what I do about writer's block. I never get it. I write really fast and it comes easy."[32] And yet, he insists, that is no way to live. "I have so little time," Stine complained. "I mean, I'm going nuts. Who in their right mind would try writing two novels a month?"[33]

Working on a book for one series at a time, he experiences no difficulty in making the transition from one series to another—though *Goosebumps* is "shorter and much less gory and violent than *Fear Street*, which is set in the mythical town of

Shadyside,"[34] where many teens are killed at the local high school.

He believes one reason he can work so rapidly is that he outlines all the action of every chapter of every book and does all of his real thinking in the outline. He *has to* outline, he comments, to make sure his books make sense.

A Lot is Luck

Stine's success notwithstanding, Holly Pupino reports that some of his story proposals have been returned "with such comments as 'Bob, psychotic rambling' or 'Bob, take a break.' He always trusts and never overrules his editors' opinion: 'One of them, after all, is my wife.'"[35]

What kind of editor is his wife? "Ruthless," Stine told Fred Kaplan in 1995. "She insists that everything makes sense," adding after a pause, "I hate that."[36]

Referring to his ability to keep producing manuscripts at high volume, he modestly insists, "A lot of it is luck. . . . I never have a day when I can't sit down and write, and some days it's awful, but you just keep going and go back and fix it."[37] Moreover, the author, who needs—and finds—two book ideas a month, says that when he started writing *Goosebumps,* he really thought there were only five story lines.

Elaborating about his apparent immunity to writer's block, he says, "This isn't bragging. And I don't think it's talent. I think it's just luck. I can always sit down and write, and I'm very disciplined. So far I've been so lucky. Whenever I need an idea I get one."[38]

Although he has sometimes denied knowing where his ideas come from, in an online website chat, he said that ideas come from everywhere. One likely source is young people. According to writer Pupino, Stine "likes to hang out with kids . . . has been known to spy on his son, Matthew, and his son's friends and then incorporate their names, mannerisms and tastes in music and clothing into his stories. Now [in 1996] that Matthew is 16 and an age-appropriate subject for *Fear Street,* Stine has taken to spying on two eight-year-old nephews for *Goosebumps* inspiration."[39] Also, of course, Stine draws on his own childhood fears.

Stine, shown here taking a break from his work, stated that two sources of his creativity are young people and books.

His reading has stimulated him, too. Stine remembered Robert Sheckley's story, *Mindswap,* when he wrote a *Goosebumps* tale about an unhappy boy who goes to a company that will switch his mind into another body. When a bee flies into the machine, the boy's brain is dispatched into the bee's body, and the boy is trapped inside the insect. Stine called the book *Why I'm Afraid of Bees.*

The germ of an idea for a Stine book might be something the author mentally pictures, such as a father with leaves instead of hair growing out of his head (*Stay Out of the Basement*), or something he actually sees, such as green slime on his son's wall (the first *Monster Blood* book). Even a family trip can provide inspiration. One such visit, to the Tower of London, gave rise to *A Night in Terror Tower,* in which a brother and sister get lost in a British castle, are separated from their parents, and face time travel, rats, and a mysterious caped man.

No One Is More En-Titled

Unlike most writers, who start with an idea, Stine starts with a title and lets his imagination run as he works out a story.

"Sometimes I'll get a title like *The Baby-Sitter*," he explains. "Then I'll think about what scary things could happen to a baby-sitter. What if she's baby-sitting in a creepy old house and gets a scary phone call?"[40] Stine's approach to *Cry of the Cat*, a *Goosebumps* book published in early 1998, provides another example of the process:

> First I thought up the title, then I got an image of a house full of crying cats and a girl who lived there. Then I imagined another girl, riding a bike, who runs over a cat and takes it to the house because she figures it must live there. And that's how the book started.[41]

While ideas always seem to come to him, Stine is unable to create a story without a title. In fact, he regards the title as so important that if he has a story and no title, he will discard the story. That may seem radical, but Stine's attitude is that failure to produce a good title immediately means that he never will come up with the right one, in which case it is pointless to continue. Stine, whose favorite *Goosebumps* title was *Legend of the Lost*

A scene from A Night in Terror Tower. *The story was inspired by a trip that the Stine family took to the Tower of London.*

Legend, wanted to name another book *Smelly Summer,* but that title was changed to *Horror at Camp Jellyjam.* In 1996 Stine quipped to an interviewer, "I have this great title: *'The Good, the Bad, the Itchy.'* I'm looking for a story. I'll think of something."[42]

Once he has a title, Stine works backward, first devising the ending and then plotting ways to fool his readers and keep them guessing.

There's one certainty about how a Stine book will *end*—and that's not in a bad way. Writer Rose Kennedy reported that he once made the mistake of having a bad ending, in *Best Friend,* a *Fear Street* book: "In it, the bad girl wins. But kids were furious! They didn't want me to leave it like that. In *Best Friend 2,* there's a chance for the ending to work out differently."[43] In fact, he told another writer, having the evil girl win in the end was so unpopular, "I actually got hate mail from kids, insisting that I write a sequel and make it a happy ending. I was so surprised that so many kids would write."[44]

It has been suggested that Stine's goofy conclusions and ironic twists diminish the scare factor in his books. Writer Tom Collins offers as an example *One Day at Horrorland,* the story of a family detoured to the amusement park from hell, which is run by monsters who take sadistic pleasure in frightening their visitors. When the Horrorland monsters close in, the heroine pinches them in the arms, which causes them to deflate. Says Collins, "This is Stine's multi-million trade secret: mix elements of horror into a premise that's too wacky to really frighten a child."[45]

As Scary and Safe as a Roller Coaster

Stine is often asked to discuss the guidelines he follows in writing his horror books. Here is what he told one interviewer: "I try to write about real kids, very normal, believable kids they [readers] can identify with. Then I put these totally believable kids into totally outlandish, scary situations. But there's never any violence—no one gets killed or hurt—and there's always a lot of humor."[46]

While Stine wants his characters to be real, he avoids putting them in situations that too closely mirror real-life horrors. "I'm very careful not to make them too real," he says. "I would never do child abuse. I'd never do drugs. I'd never do suicide. They're just too real, they're not any fun."[47] Divorce is another subject avoided by Stine, who considers the real world much more frightening than what he writes about. In fact, Stine feels that scary stories help children cope with a frightening world. According to one writer, "What they're looking for, Stine believes, is examples of other kids who, even though frightened, overcome fear through their own strength and resourcefulness."[48]

In support of this observation, the author reports that a troubled preteen recited a plot of one of Stine's books each week when she visited a child psychologist. The psychologist believed that the child was developing the ability to master her real fears by facing the fictional ones.

Essentially, however, Stine emphasizes that his books are meant just to entertain and, having written for kids for so long, he knows how far he can go and what not to do. Accordingly, he

A Jovial Announcement

The birth of the Stines' son was announced in a spirit typical of the baby's father. The cover of the birth announcement reads, "Jane and Bob Stine jovially announce the birth on June 7, 1980 of Matthew Daniel Stine" . . . and inside, next to a photo of the proud parents and the infant (in a bunny outfit) "a wild and crazy baby!!"

Early on, Matt and his dad did a lot of fun things together such as exploring New York City, visiting the Museum of Natural History, watching Laurel and Hardy movies and playing ball. Later, they shared frequent trips to Disney World.

But there was one surprise. Unlike most kids in America, Matthew Stine had read either none (as R. L. Stine once contended) or just one of his father's books. "I don't like to read," Matthew told reporter Mary B. W. Tabor. "I write music and play guitar." According to Tabor, the only Stine book Matthew had read featured a protagonist modeled and named after him, who is bitten by his vampire girlfriend. Matt also posed for the cover of *The Perfect Date*, a *Fear Street* book.

Discussing his son's refusal to read his books, Stine told Paul Higbie, a young Connecticut interviewer, "He brags about it. He knows it makes me crazy." Jane Stine concurs. When Matt was fifteen, she told newswriter Paul Lomartire, "It's a point of honor with Matt [not reading his father's books]. I think he does it to annoy Bob, and it works."

avoids incorporating any serious theme that would interfere with the entertainment. While he wants to scare his readers, Stine emphasizes, "I'm not interested in terrifying children. I'm interested in entertaining kids. I see it all as funny. Maybe it's my twisted sense of humor, but at the end of every chapter is a cliffhanger line. I see it as a kind of punch line. I like writing jokes."[49]

Writer James Kaplan points out that Stine's works are based on the premise that kids love to be safely scared by such phenomena as zombies, monsters, and haunted cuckoo clocks. "Stine's books," he continues, "put their young heroes and heroines in harm's way but never harm them, and contain jokes and gross-outs galore."[50] Almost always, good triumphs over evil.

Stine feels that one appealing aspect of his books is that "while you're reading about monsters and phantoms and weird creatures, you're safe in your home. It's nice and safe, and you know the books are going to end up nice and safe. So it's safe to be scared."[51]

He likens his books' "safe scares" to a roller-coaster ride, during which riders are biting their knuckles and holding on for dear life, but land without mishap. "You know how it is going to end before you get on. It's a fast, exciting ride that lets you off safe and sound at the end," he emphasizes. "The books have the same kind of thrill."[52] Consequently, he considers his books reassuring to the army of readers who like to be frightened while feeling confident of their personal safety. Writer Vivian Rose reported that one mother wrote Stine: "I appreciate that you give my kid shivers, not nightmares."[53]

Home Work, Nice Work

Stine does his writing in a room of his Upper West Side apartment in New York City, where the decor in a recent year included a plastic skeleton, a pinball machine, a knife with an eight-inch blade, and a plastic finger cut off at the knuckle. On the wall a 1920s poster showed a woman hunched over a Remington typewriter. He was planning to buy a pool table. "Pool's a good game when you're getting old," he told a reporter. "[You] don't need special sneakers."[54]

Stine, seen here with props from The Haunted Mask, *would watch Saturday morning cartoons and read children's books to ensure that his stories remained current.*

Usually with his dog, Nadine (a little white King Charles spaniel named after a Chuck Berry song), at his feet, Stine works from about 9 in the morning until 3:30 or 4 in the afternoon, with time out to eat lunch and walk the dog in nearby Central Park. Stine and his wife go to ballet and opera performances at Lincoln Center. Fond of old black-and-white movies and a dedicated viewer of televised football games, he'd watch Saturday morning cartoons and reads children's books and magazines. "I

What-Not Plots

"The unwritten rules for these books are clear," writes David Wilkison in the *Cleveland Plain Dealer*. "There is no blood and gore, nobody gets seriously hurt, and any death—say, of a witch who has temporarily turned the town's adults into appleheads—is discreet."

Another newsman, Andrew Billen, makes a similar observation: "The books are creepy fantasies: kids become invisible and don't know how to get back, mummies come to life, schools are haunted. But there is not much violence in *Goosebumps*."

Within these parameters, Stine's plots are all over the horror map—from one in which everyone but the hero's brother becomes invisible (*Let's Get Invisible!*) to one in which a cocker spaniel eats monster blood and grows as big as a pony (*Monster Blood II*) to books in which ventriloquist dummies come alive (*Night of the Living Dummy* and its sequels).

There are stories in which such ordinary situations as a summer at sleepaway camp (*Ghost Camp*), studying a musical instrument (*Piano Lessons Can Be Murder*), being photographed (*Say Cheese and Die!* and its sequel), or a class trip (*Deep in the Jungle of Doom*) take on eerie, frightening qualities.

Perhaps unsurprisingly, Stine, who made almost weekly journeys to the barbershop to read "literature" banned from his home, has a book entitled *My Hairiest Adventure*. Here a boy opens a bottle of Instant Tan but, instead of getting a tan, he sprouts hair on his hands and knees like a hairy monster. And in *Vampire Breath*, a boy and girl, exploring a secret basement room, open a bottle and release a very thirsty vampire.

Sometimes the theme is vengeance (*fowl* play?), as in *Chicken Chicken*, touted as a "finger-lickin' nightmare," in which a girl who wears black lipstick and is known as "Weird Vanessa" turns kids who are rude to her into chickens.

have to keep up," he explains. "I can't sound like some guy from Mars who doesn't know what's going on."[55]

Commenting that he loves working at home, he joked in an online website chat, "When I finish work in the afternoon, I don't have to go home. I'm already there."[56] But in a serious vein, Stine declared in a newspaper interview in 1995:

I really love writing. I enjoy doing it so much, so I have my own pressure to keep going, to keep producing the series. And then I have so many people depending on me now. . . . This is not for humans, doing this many books, but I'm suited for it. I love being at home. I love being by myself all day thinking up new plots. I love it.[57]

Obviously, scores of admirers love what Stine is doing, too.

Chapter 5

Popularity: "No One Comes Close"

O NLY FIVE YEARS after the launch of his *Fear Street* series, Stine became the nation's best-selling author, surpassing prolific novelists Stephen King, John Grisham, and Tom Clancy. One week in 1994, there were 30 Stine titles on *USA Today*'s list of 234 best-sellers in all categories, not just children's books. And when 26 Stine titles appeared on its list of the year's 150 best-selling books of 1995, the newspaper commented: "In sheer number of volumes sold, no one comes close to R. L. Stine." [58]

Stine's works appeared consistently on the best-seller lists of such publications as the *New York Times* and *Publishers Weekly*, which named him the number-one best-selling author for three consecutive years (1994, 1995, and 1996). It was rare that a Stine book did not make the list.

One indication of just how popular Stine's books have been: *Goosebumps* sales totaled about 35 million in the first three years of publication, while the classic *Nancy Drew* mystery series took 65 years to reach 80 million. By 1994 his books were being shipped at the rate of 1.25 million a month, and quickly selling out, in time for the next book to hit the stands and repeat the process. Not surprisingly, as Stine has told his fans, he finds it very exciting to go into a bookstore and see so many shelves filled with his books.

As of October 1996 an astounding 4.5 million Stine books were sold monthly—more than enough, according to one observer, to supply a book to every nine-year-old in America.

Stine's popularity extends beyond U.S. borders, with distribution agreements involving *Goosebumps* in twenty nations and translations into at least sixteen languages, including Chinese, Czech, and Spanish. Noting that his books had been translated into Hebrew, Stine quipped in an interview, "My mother said I'd finally done something right."[59]

Stine repeatedly contracted to write more books at the same furious pace, and, by spring of 1999, 300 million copies of his *Fear Street* and *Goosebumps* series had been sold in the United States. *Goosebumps*, the best-selling children's book series of all time, had more than 200 million copies still in print, and *Fear Street* (including *Ghosts of Fear Street*) was the nation's most popular series of teen paperbacks, selling more than 43 million copies of 120 titles. *Goosebumps* books (including *Goosebumps Series 2000*, introduced in January 1998) became the best-selling children's series in several foreign countries, including England, France, and Australia, and the Sunday *Times* of London cited a library survey in which Stine's books were reported to be the most-borrowed items by children in the United Kingdom.

Stine even made *Entertainment Weekly*'s list of the 101 most powerful people in entertainment in 1996. He was rated number 100.

Beyond the Numbers

Beyond the numbers, there is strong evidence of Stine's immense popularity. Many children boast of owning the entire *Goosebumps* series, and some youngsters sort the books by subject (e.g., alien, mummy, monster blood). Stine's increasingly rare appearances at book fairs and stores caused massive traffic jams.

Fan clubs and book clubs popped up everywhere, many with their own special gimmicks. For example, seven Barnes & Noble booksellers in Florida began holding monthly *Goosebumps* book club meetings, and naming September and October "*Goosebumps* Haunting Season." At the stores, kids could pick up a special "haunting license" and be entered in drawings for tickets to a museum and zoo. In the chain's clubs in California,

meetings included readings and discussions of the latest ghoul-
ish novel and such *Goosebumps*-themed activities as wrapping a
mummy and writing letters to Stine. At the Barnes & Noble store
in Santa Monica, California, supervisor Charlotte Wildberger,
who read the books to children at monthly meetings, said that
youngsters asked for the new *Goosebumps* before the ink had
dried on the previous one. Other bookstores across the country
formed clubs, offering members newsletters, discounts on books
and merchandise, and previews of forthcoming book covers.
Some conducted contests, such as "Draw Your Own *Goosebumps*
Cover." At one club, a $10.95 membership bought a water bot-
tle, a watch, a scarf, and a membership card, all delivered in a
miniature coffin.

Publishers who had not previously taken the children's book
market seriously, certainly do now, thanks to Stine. The first
horror series for children has had a tremendous impact on the
publishing industry.

One of the biggest surprises, and a possible key to Stine's
success, has been that his two series appeal to both genders.
When the mail from young readers to Stine started coming in,
there was a shocking discovery: 50 percent of the fan mail was
from boys. This result is contrary to the widely held belief in
publishing that girls read but boys do not. Perhaps Stine has
both male and female fans partly because his main characters
are both boys and girls.

Grown-Up Horror

In view of the overwhelming success of Stine's horror books for
young readers, it seemed logical, at least to some observers, that
he could score a triumph with a similar type of book for the
adult market.

Yet, when the opportunity arose, his initial reaction was not to
take it. But ultimately the million-dollar offer and the chance to
work with a major entertainment world figure were too appealing
to turn down. As Stine recalls in a conversation with Fred Kaplan,
"One day, I'm sitting here, and Brandon Tartikoff [who was a
powerful entertainment industry executive] calls and says, 'I'd like

A scene from director Alfred Hitchcock's horror movie Psycho. *Stine was hesitant at first when asked to write a horror story for adults.*

you to write an adult horror story.' I say, 'No thanks, go away.' I think he was shocked. Not too many writers say no to Brandon Tartikoff."[60] According to Stine's account, Tartikoff persisted, explaining that he had an imprint, or publishing subdivision, of Warner Books and was contracting four or five books a year, all with book-movie tie-ins. Stine could write any book he wanted and Tartikoff would produce the movie.

Stine agreed to a meeting and, despite his initial reluctance, embarked in 1995 on a horror novel for adults, *Superstitious.* The title materialized when his son asked him whether he knew the Stevie Wonder song "Superstitious," and Stine knew that would be his title (although the song is actually "Superstit*ion*"). Set in a

Brandon Tartikoff (pictured) asked Stine to write a story that could be made into a motion picture.

small Pennsylvania college town, *Superstitious* was a story about a professor of Irish folklore, a female graduate student, and a series of gruesome murders. Stine set the story at a college because it seemed to him a logical progression from high school, where his *Fear Street* books take place.

Why was the main character Irish? Stine concedes, "I don't know from Irish. But my wife has a crush on [Irish-born] Daniel Day-Lewis, and she said, 'I don't care what you write about, but Daniel Day-Lewis has to star in the movie.'"[61] According to Mary B. W. Tabor, the book has some sex scenes and some foul language, "but the writing, which is clipped and heavy with thump-thump-thump, dark creatures in the shadows, cliffhanger chapters and a surprise ending, is classic Stine." The author described the book to Tabor as "horrible," "awful," "gruesome, really." Then, chuckling, he added, "I can't believe you read it."[62] On other occasions, he has laughingly evaluated his adult work as gross or hideous, no doubt the effects he seeks.

Several reviewers panned the book, which had taken Stine four months to write. *Publishers Weekly* described the suspense story as having "crude yet functional casting, plotting and prose." A *Washington Post* critic called *Superstitious* "not a good book." "The *Post* just killed me," Stine told interviewer Fred Kaplan. "The guy who did it wrote a really good, thoughtful review, too." Then, after a pause, he said with a laugh, "I hate that sort of thing." [63]

Stine claimed not to be surprised at the negative critical reaction. As he told Mary Tabor, "I sort of expected to get killed in reviews. Nobody wants a children's book writer to switch over, especially one as successful as I am. Also, I have a lot to learn. I don't expect to be Stephen King immediately." [64]

Despite the negative reviews, the novel published by Warner Books sold 150,000 hardcover copies, quite a respectable figure compared with almost anything but one of the *Goosebumps* books. And he sold the movie rights to his book to Miramax.

"He isn't contemplating writing another [adult book]," comments a reporter. "He didn't enjoy it very much— too much real world in there." [65] Stine acknowledges it is a strain to be reality based.

Throughout the *Superstitious* project, Stine remained heavily involved in writing for young readers. As 1997 came to an end, he slightly shifted *Goosebumps* gears, moving from the standard series (which had sixty-two titles) to *Goosebumps Series 2000*. "We're not really making it *more* scary," he said at the time. "We're adding scares; same kind, only more. We were getting so much mail from kids, saying 'I've read 40 or 50 of your books but I want more,' that we decided to . . . add more scares and heighten the danger." [66] The new series, which has the same humor but is more unpredictable and more detailed, led off in early 1998 with *Cry of the Cat,* in which a girl encounters a mysterious, evil cat that refuses to stay dead, followed by *Bride of the Living Dummy* and *Creature Teacher.*

Stine comments that whenever he has asked young readers whether they thought a book was scary, the inevitable response is that it isn't scary enough. Thus, the new series, which he said was treading a fine line—adding a little to the fright-and-danger quotient, but keeping the books in the *Goosebumps* tradition.

A License to Frighten

As is often the case with a successful commodity, the *Goosebumps* books gave rise to a host of licensed products, everything from back-to-school products (notebooks, folders, pencils, Ghost-It notes, and more) to a Milton Bradley board game called "Terror in the Graveyard," in which trapped players can escape only by depositing a skull in a crypt and to win must defeat a headless ghost. Kenner Products produced a *Goosebumps* toy line that included edible "brains" in three delicious flavors. There were also home videos, sleeping bags, tattoos, stickers, flashlights, paper hats, banners and balloons, trading cards, and an interactive CD-ROM game. Walt Disney Records and Scholastic marketed *Goosebumps* audiotapes with sound effects, a musical score, and such performers as Nancy Cartwright, heard as the voice of Bart Simpson on *The Simpsons* television series. By late 1996, more than forty licenses had been issued to companies in the United States and abroad.

Scholastic Productions and Parachute Press introduced a line of children's sporting goods inspired by *Goosebumps,* while Seneca Sports produced in-line skates, skateboards, and protective gear, and Great Scott developed several *Goosebumps*-licensed lines: winter sports equipment, bike accessories, and outdoor sports products.

What may have been the most elaborate—and surely most controversial—tie-in was a $40 million agreement involving Stine, Scholastic, and several PepsiCo divisions. The agreement called for Stine to create three 32-page "thrillogy" books that would not be available in bookstores. Instead, youngsters would obtain them by unsealing a bag of Doritos chips, sending in coupons from Pepsi twelve-packs or big bottles, or clipping newspaper ads for Hershey Foods products.

Pepsi was to distribute coupons on more than 40 million packs and bottles; its Frito-Lay unit would package the miniature books in more than 30 million bags of various products, and

Hershey would run newspaper inserts aimed at 52 million households. There were also collectible cups, which customers could take to Toys "R" Us stores and redeem for books.

While Scholastic officials emphasized that the books did not endorse any particular product and that PepsiCo had no influence on the editorial content, some consumers were offended by the books' links to "junk food." Kathryn Montgomery, president of the Center for Media Education, declares: "Obviously you want to give them credit for promoting reading. [But] I find the merger of promotion and content troubling."[67] More emphatic was Michael Jacobson, executive director of the Center for Science in the Public Interest, who called it "disgusting that kids are encouraged to buy junk food to get these specially prepared books."[68]

But Mary Somerville, then president-elect of the American Library Association, applauded Pepsi's plans, according to reporter Lisa L. Brownlee. "There are always questions with advertising to children, who are vulnerable," Somerville said. "But . . . getting kids

"Sorry to Hear You're Deceased"

At one point, the popularity of Stine's books was such that fan letters came in at the rate of two thousand or more a week, too many for him to read all. But, with help, he made sure that every letter writer got an answer, if only a form reply.

"Half the kids who write to me say they want to be horror writers when they grow up," Stine commented to writer John Kiesewetter. "So I think we're in for some very scary times."

Some of the fan-letter writers are parents. The mother of one *Goosebumps* enthusiast wanted Stine to know that "I'm completely supportive of [his] reading 'addiction' because he is profoundly deaf and reading is his door to the world. The *Goosebumps* books stimulate [his] senses through his imagination, and make him feel like a normal kid because being a *Goosebumps* fan is an experience he shares with lots of other kids."

Of the thousands of letters Stine has received from young fans, several are particularly memorable, including one reporting, "I've read 40 of your books, and I think they're really boring."

Then there are those that deal with rumors of his retirement or even passing. Journalist Joyce M. Rosenberg reported that a fan wrote, "Sorry to hear you're deceased," while another, more patient one, asked, "Can I take over your series when you die?"

to read anything—even a cereal box—is a step in the right direction." Somerville also made the point that Stine's project was not the first use of books for a cross-promotion. Before the turn of the century, she said, pioneer children in the Midwest "learned to read through a series of books produced by a flour company."[69]

Only a Matter of Time

It was only a matter of time before *Goosebumps* would take to the airwaves, although, despite the books' immense popularity, getting TV network executives to accept *Goosebumps* was not easy. Deborah Forte, executive producer of the series for Scholastic Productions, recalls, "They said it will never work . . . anthologies don't work." But while acknowledging that networks prefer programs with a continuing cast of characters, she notes that ultimately, "we decided to go with our vision."[70]

In the fall of 1995, the Fox Children's Network (now known as the Fox Kids Network) went with that vision on TV, running an hour-long Halloween-theme *Goosebumps* episode called "The Haunted Mask," based on the book of the same name. The episode features Carly Beth, a shy, easily frightened eleven-year-old who is tormented by two male classmates. In a dusty novelty shop run by a nameless, scarred man, Carly buys a horrifying Halloween mask that she hopes will scare the boys, but the mask has strange powers and will not come off.

The idea for the book, *The Haunted Mask*, originally came to Stine from a real-life experience. One Halloween, his son Matt put on a green rubber Frankenstein mask and then, as much as he tugged, could not get it off. "I suppose I should have helped him remove it," Stine says in his autobiography, "but instead I ran to my desk and started writing notes. I knew it would make a great plot for a story!"[71] And, remembering how embarrassed he had been by the duck costume he wore every Halloween, the author gave Carly Beth one.

Launching the Series

A party to launch the live-action series was held in a nightclub, a former church decorated with skeletons, caskets, and spider

Two masks from The Haunted Mask *are seen here. Stine's television specials were so popular that they ran in the time period formerly occupied by the* Mighty Morphin Power Rangers.

webs. Greeting several hundred fans who'd been invited there to a screening was Stine, dressed in black, a frequent choice. As the mild-mannered author once explained to a reporter, "The kids want to meet someone more like Dracula."[77]

When dressed in black, Stine, who has mournful dark eyes under thick eyebrows, *can* appear rather somber, and, in some poses, might not look out of place in a laboratory creating a monster. But the author, who has been described as resembling comic actor Jon Lovitz, only taller and trimmer, has an easy smile and a ready laugh. He is not at all sinister or menacing, as his books or TV show might suggest.

The hour-long TV special scored high in the ratings, and Fox decided to schedule weekly half-episodes based on Stine's books, to run in the time period that had been occupied by the popular *Mighty Morphin Power Rangers.* Over the next three seasons, Fox would run half a dozen prime-time specials in addition to the weekly episodes. A prime-time special in the second year, *Haunted Mask II,* had the boy who had been frightened by Carly Beth seeking his own especially scary mask. He finds one in the same spooky store and buys it from the same wrinkled man. As expected, the boy's mask has unusual powers.

The Thrillmaster Is Thrilled

Stine himself did not write the scripts for the TV series, but, as consultant, he got to review them. He was thrilled with such weekly episodes as "It Came from Beneath the Sink," about a kitchen sponge that comes to life; "The Cuckoo Clock of Doom," in which a boy gets his wish that his obnoxious kid sister had never been born; "Piano Lessons Can Be Murder," about a music student haunted by a ghost; "Say Cheese and Die!," in which a camera becomes a family curse; and "Bad Hare Day," about a stagestruck boy who is delighted when a magician turns him into a rabbit.

Noting that the TV series had come about in response to demand from readers, Stine said he was optimistic that, rather than serving as an alternative to reading, it would encourage the activity. "My hope," he added in a newspaper interview, "is that we'll

Two children are seen here acting in a Goosebumps *television special.*

have maybe a million more kids reading at night under the blankets."[73] The TV show apparently had the desired effect. In June 1996, Stine was able to report that since the TV show began, sales of his books had jumped considerably. And he was very proud of the fact that many more children were now reading.

They might have been scared into it. Despite elements of humor and irony, *Goosebumps* scripts had been given a cautionary GB-7 rating indicating that the content might be inappropriate for children age seven or younger. But Deborah Forte, sounding a familiar theme, pointed out, "We are very careful never to refer to it as the horror genre because traditionally, horror has meant more violent, gory stories. We make the analogy that *Goosebumps* is a roller-coaster ride rather than a house of horrors. We call the series 'safe scares' because there is no violence and no real life threats."[74]

Developing the Show

In developing the show, Forte said, Scholastic Productions officials had realized that many children were watching shows not necessarily intended for them. With *Goosebumps*, Scholastic tried to create high-quality programs that didn't necessarily have happy endings but did respect the audience's intelligence. Writing about one *Goosebumps* show, James Kaplan observes, "Like all the episodes, it is technically superb, funny and scary in equal measures, fast-paced and compelling. It has to be." Kaplan goes on to note that, "Since the shows are more explicitly visual than the books, there are a number of ironclad rules: no blood, no violence, no real-world physical threats."[75]

Susan Young writes in the *Oakland Tribune:*

> Stine knows how to build tension into his finely woven stories, which makes the shows enjoyable for both kids and adults. Stine's formula takes ordinary kids, puts them into supernatural situations and whips up some macabre mischief. His talent is in making these stories genuinely scary without creating a generation of insomniacs. He accomplishes that by tempering the tales with a generous helping of humor.[76]

In this scene from Goosebumps, *two children peer into the darkness. The series features "safe scares" in which there are no violent acts or life-threatening events.*

Success on Television

In Stine's opinion, the TV shows were successful for the same reason the books were successful: they were not truly terrifying and they pulled back with humor when things got really scary.

After the series had run for three successive seasons as the top-rated children's show in the United States, it was picked up again by Fox and ran until December 1998.

Producer/director Tim Burton (*Mars Attacks, Beetlejuice, Edward Scissorhands,* and *Batman*) agreed to produce a feature film version of *Goosebumps,* to be based on a combination of the characters, story lines, and tone of the sixty-two book series. Beyond film, "Goosebumps Live," a stage show produced by Feld Entertainment (Ringling Brothers, Barnum & Bailey Circus), toured the United States in 1998 and the United Kingdom in 1999.

TV was also a good avenue for *Fear Street.* In 1997 ABC-TV announced a new pilot, *The Ghosts of Fear Street,* which Stine described to reporter Susy Schultz as "not a sitcom, but . . . sort of a frightcom—funny and scary."[77] *Fear Street* was moving ahead on other fronts, too. A feature film was in the works, and in October 1997, Golden Books Family Entertainment acquired the rights to publish sixty-five new *Fear Street* titles under the joint imprint of Parachute and Golden. There would be a new story line called *Seniors: A Fear Street Series,* covering the adventures of the senior class at Shadyside High. A feature film and a TV series based on the books were reportedly due soon, as well.

The *Goosebumps* TV series was also popular overseas. Produced in Canada by Protocol Entertainment in association with Scholastic Productions, it was one of the top ten shows in that country in 1996. The series was sold to the Canadian French-language broadcaster, Canal Famille, with thirty episodes of "Chair de Poule" (which means "goosebumps" in French—literally "chicken flesh").

Famous producer and director Tim Burton (pictured) agreed to produce the film version of Goosebumps.

Back in the United States, rentals of *Goosebumps* videos were flourishing; for the week ending September 22, 1996, three of the episodes were among the top ten family video rentals from Blockbuster Entertainment.

Goosebumps Goes to Disneyland

"I'm so excited, I'll have my own land at MGM," Stine declared in a 1997 newspaper interview. "It'll have a live show, a fun house and *Goosebumps* gift shop."[78] The author was reacting to the news that his books had inspired a new attraction at Disney-MGM Studios in Orlando, Florida: The Goosebumps HorrorLand Fright Show and Fun House. Stine made plans to spend Halloween night at HorrorLand, which opened in October 1997 featuring creepy *Goosebumps* characters who interact with guests onstage. Bats, werewolves, and snakes were among the inhabitants.

Imitation may be the sincerest form of flattery, but not always the most tasteful. Parodies of *Goosebumps* included such offerings as the books in the *Barforama* series, which featured such titles as *Mucus Mansion, Garbage Time* and *The Great Pukeoff;* the repulsive-looking covers carried the words "Warning! Guaranteed Gross-Out!" The publisher, Bantam Doubleday Dell, offered readers a $5.50 membership in the Barf-O-Rama Club, which entitled them to "get lots of disgustingly cool stuff," including fake cockroaches and two issues of *The Gross Gazette.*

Another publisher's *Gooflumps,* by "R. U. Slime," included spoofs of Stine's *Stay Out of the Basement* (which it called *Gooflumps 2 1/2: Stay Out of the Bathroom*), and one that poked fun at Stine's *Say Cheese and Die* (which it titled *Gooflumps 4 1/2: Eat Cheese and Barf*). Among copycat series and books were *The Bug Files, Tales from the Crypt, Slimeballs,* and *Graveyard School.*

Some yuck-inspiring spinoffs came from the *Goosebumps* publisher. For instance, in 1997 Scholastic Books presented a children's scratch-and-sniff calendar with thirteen "totally gross scratch and stinky smells—includes dog breath, rotten eggs, sweaty socks, and more!" The back of the calendar contained a Stinky Smells Answer Key for anyone who couldn't identify a

Drop in Popularity

The tidal wave of popularity enjoyed by Stine's books could not be expected to peak indefinitely. In 1997 Scholastic announced it would lose money in the third quarter mainly because bookstores were returning *Goosebumps* titles at a higher rate than expected. When it became known that so many unsold books were being sent back, with resulting disappointing third-quarter figures, the value of a share of the company's stock dropped almost by half.

The horror stories, whose popularity surged in recent years among preteens, accounted for half of Scholastic's retail books sales, the company said in a news release, adding that the series was "the victim of its own expansion. Parents have stopped buying the older titles as new titles and products have proliferated." As reported by William Flannery in the *St. Louis Post-Dispatch* on February 22, 1997, Richard Robinson, Scholastic president and chief executive, said, "The reduced sales of older *Goosebumps* titles came a bit sooner than we had planned."

Stine was not surprised at the decline in sales. He told Susy Schultz, of the *Chicago Sunday Sun-Times*, "We were selling between 3 and 4 million books a month. So it didn't come as a shock when things slowed down. It had to happen sometime, but nobody could predict when it would level off."

particular unpleasant odor. Awful puns were another feature. National Skeleton Month (November) asked: "Why do skeletons laugh so much?" "Because they have funny bones!" There were also spinoff book serials: *Give Yourself Goosebumps*, in which readers could choose the story ending, and *Goosebumps Presents*, based on the TV shows, which themselves were based on the original books. Introduced in 1995, the spinoffs were reportedly selling at almost the same rate as the originals. Meanwhile, on *Fear Street*, the plan was for *Monster Blood III* to be sold with a packet of green, gooey—what else?—monster blood.

Not that sales really needed any kind of transfusion. But along with imitators and sincere admirers of Stine's works, there were equally sincere critics, the severest of whom were themselves "out for blood."

Chapter 6

Mild-Mannered Center of a Storm

CONTROVERSY SURROUNDING HORROR books is nothing new, but the level of passion inspired by Stine's works seems to be especially intense. Some critics mounted campaigns to ban them. In the 1800s, lurid popular tales called "penny dreadfuls," a name reflecting both price and content, stirred similar cries. And even such tame children's series as *Nancy Drew* and *The Hardy Boys* have been criticized or ignored by librarians for lack of the right moral stuff. Stine's books, likewise, have been alternately praised and condemned by educators and parents.

Many like his books just for their ability to encourage otherwise reluctant children, boys especially, to become dedicated readers. The books' easy-to-read style, simple language, and gross, frightening content are major factors here. The hope of many was that readers of Stine's works would "graduate" to reading books that were more sophisticated and of higher quality.

Others condemn the works, sometimes on the very grounds that some praise them. Occasionally, for instance, the publisher of *Goosebumps* gets a letter asking how it can publish such nightmare-inspiring books. One standard response, according to Scholastic executive Jean Feiwel, is that the books are "a refuge, and they're not real in any way. And . . . to kids' lives, which are dominated by true horror, I think these books represent a total escape."[79]

Many young *Goosebumps* readers seem to agree. Says one: "I really like them because they're not so scary that they give you nightmares, but they're scary enough. And they're funny." Reporter Don O'Briant also quotes another fan: "It's fun to be scared when you know you're not in danger."[80] The feeling is echoed by other readers, one of whom cited by another reporter, calls Stine's books "really suspenseful. They're not actually scary scary but they keep you on your toes."[81]

In Stine's view, his books, in which children escape suspenseful jams by using their wits, have another value: "In real life, children are often powerless. They are told what to do by their parents, teachers, older brothers and sisters, and other adults. In the *Goosebumps* world, children have power."[82]

"Parents seem to be really pleased, especially because their boys are reading," says Carl Wichman, book specialist of Fargo, North Dakota's Media Play, who comments that Stine is "very good at coming up with today's language for the kids. Today's styles, backgrounds, clothing . . . you name it, it's all there." Wichman goes on to say, "You hope for more quality, but get them into *Goosebumps* and maybe in the future they'll pick up Agatha Christie or Edgar Allan Poe."[83]

Similar sentiments are expressed by other observers. "I'd rather kids read good literature than less good literature, but kids aren't reading a whole lot these days,"[84] notes UCLA education professor Deborah Stipek. Another faint-praise observation comes from Ramona Mahood, an assistant professor at the University of Memphis, who specializes in children's literature: "They may not be the best books, but there's no sex, no graphic violence and no four-letter words. . . . My philosophy is that kids are better off reading than not reading."[85] Stine himself urges fans not to limit their reading to his books.

Various educators advise that parents monitor the books. Some parents who read books with their children and approach Stine's works expecting to be repelled are pleasantly surprised. Rita Hathaway of Minnetonka, Minnesota, for one, says she was "not thrilled" with the books' concept. But when she and her husband read them, they found the content was not "as bad as the covers. . . . I view them as the preferred choice to no books." Like others, the Hathaways also believe that the scary parts stop at the covers. Their young children are "enthralled" [and] "think reading can be fun and interesting." Another Minnetonka mother, Mary Moulton, who liked being scared when she was a child, screens not only her children's reading but their television and movie viewing. Moulton comments: "You go with the culture, or they stop reading. Lots of kids who don't read *Goosebumps* are watching 'Terminator' movies. I think literature is better than movies like that."[86]

Parents often find that by reading the books aloud with their children, answering questions, and explaining what was going on, they can lower the "scare quotient." Some parents go further: "I think [the books are] good for the kids," says Sandra Gillett, mother of at least one *Goosebumps* reader. "There's always a logical explanation for everything; it helps kids get over their own fears."[87]

Similarly, Dr. Carol Falender, chief psychologist at St. John's Child and Family Development Center, says: "Kids who are healthy and secure love [*Goosebumps*]. Other kids have nightmares, but these are kids who have probably sustained some other trauma."[88]

Could reading horror have an adverse effect on children when they grow up? Jim Trelease, author of *The Read Aloud Handbook* and an education consultant specializing in children's reading, says: "There's no connection between reading this stuff and deviant behavior as an adult. The people who grow up to become freeway killers are not reading [popular author of adult escape fiction] Judith Krantz or R. L. Stine."[89] In fact, according to Trelease, research shows that people who grow up hooked on reading serials are those with the highest grades in high school and college and the ones coming out of the nation's graduate schools.

Great If It Inspires Reading

Among the correspondence Stine cherishes is a letter from a mother who expresses gratitude for the series: "My son has never willingly read a book in his life. Then, the other night, I saw him reading one of your books at 2 A.M. with a flashlight under his covers. Thank you."[90]

"Anything that keeps them reading," says Diane Roback, children's book editor for *Publishers Weekly*, "anything that gets

Scares and the Scare-Master

The author, who still enjoys scary things but claims not to be easily scared, says he enjoys horror films. "They make me laugh," he told writer Rose Kennedy. Among the few films that frightened him were *Arachnophobia* and, at least in spots, *Jurassic Park*. Among his own works, he considers the *Fear Street Saga* books, a subgroup of the series, particularly frightening and *Night of the Living Dummy* (at the time he'd completed its first sequel) his scariest *Goosebumps*.

For scare-seekers new to the series, Stine recommends starting with *Night of the Living Dummy*. For those who do not want to be scared that much, he recommended a less-frightening work, *The Cuckoo Clock of Doom*.

He has listed his favorite *Goosebumps* as *Night of the Living Dummy*, *Stay Out of the Basement*, and *The Haunted Mask*. Among *Fear Street* titles, he cited *Silent Night* and *Silent Night II*, followed by *Switched* and *The Face*. He has less enthusiasm for some books in the *Fear Street* series, admitting in a 1994 website chat that he "was never really happy with *The Knife*."

Three young actors are shown here in a scene from the television episode The Haunted Mask II.

them excited about going into a bookstore, anything that has kids anticipating when a new *Goosebumps* comes out, I think that's great."[91]

Beth Puffer, manager of the Bank Street College bookstore in New York City, is more cautious: "There's nothing intrinsically harmful about *Goosebumps,* but if they're all your child is reading, he's missing something from his book list."[92] Some professional educators suggest that the books are poor examples for children learning to write. Also critical is a reading instructor who had fought what she came to realize was "a losing battle" to discourage her eight-year-old daughter from reading *Goosebumps:* "They are just not quality literature. They don't have the plot and the challenges as far as introducing new ideas, new concepts. . . . There's just no meat to them."[93]

Some criticism has been considerably more harsh. Katherine Kersten, chair of the Center of the American Experiment in Minneapolis, says *Goosebumps* differ from works like *Treasure Island, The Wizard of Oz,* and *Old Yeller* "in a crucial way—they induce fear, but drive out pity." According to Kersten, who also has been a commentator for National Public Radio's *All Things Considered,* readers of *Goosebumps* are "in constant fear; the books are raw catalogs of horrors, whose pasteboard characters serve merely to advance the plot from one shock to the next. Far from encouraging empathy, *Goosebumps* lead children to objectify others, and to enjoy—with morbid fascination—the spectacle of their suffering."[94]

A Horrible Thought: Ban Them

Evidence of just how strongly some object to Stine's books was apparent in September 1997 during Banned Books Week, an observance *USA Today* describes as "designed to draw attention to what a coalition of librarians, booksellers, publishers and authors, considers threats to free expression."[95] Stine, along with Mark Twain, author of *Tom Sawyer* and *Huckleberry Finn,* and African American poet-playwright Maya Angelou topped the American Library Association's list of "most challenged authors"—authors whose works libraries and schools have restricted and sometimes banned. In the number-one position was

Stine's work has been censored more than that of writers Mark Twain (top) and Maya Angelou (bottom).

Goosebumps, which at the time had about 180 million copies in print. The Office for Intellectual Freedom had recorded fourteen challenges to *Goosebumps* submitted to the American Library Association.

There has been a move to ban Stine's books in Kirkwood, Missouri, and attacks on his books have been reported in various communities, including Spokane, Washington; Evergreen, Colorado; and Lynn Haven, Florida. In January 1997 controversy surfaced in Minnesota, where Anoka-Hennepin School District 11 took up a mother's request that nine *Goosebumps* titles be banned from its schools' libraries. The mother, Margaret Byron, cited her reasons as follows: "While the books are only fiction and unreal, children under the age of 12, as well as many teenagers, may not be able to handle the frightening content of the books. Some children could become paranoid and insecure about daily life after reading the books. The book covers alone are quite offensive." Byron contended that the books treat children as "victims of horror," "have an overall evil theme," and frequently feature children who keep frightening secrets from their parents. "We as parents have the right to choose better quality reading,"[96] Byron insisted.

When a committee comprising Byron's school principal, parents, teachers, the school librarian, and other citizens failed to agree on a course of action and the books remained on the shelves,

Scary Books Are Like Rock Climbing: How Close to the Edge Can You Come?

Commenting on *Goosebumps*, Professor Michael R. Collings, English teacher and head of the creative writing program at Pepperdine University, said: "Part of their popularity is you get to read something that is supposed to be scary, but it isn't [scary] because you know the writer is in charge at all times. It's a safe way for kids to pretend they're getting scared."

Collings, who prefers that children read fairy tales, some of which have moral lessons, added: "I would generally not recommend them [*Goosebumps*] because they are not legitimately scary."

As quoted by Josh Grossberg, Collings compares reading horror stories to rock climbing.

> You see how close to the edge you can come. It energizes us and excites us. The heart beats faster. By reading a book, we can experience those highs but never be in danger.

> Life is a struggle and kids are acutely aware of that. They aren't living in as civilized a world as adults. It's more common for a kid to get beat up than an adult, and they are more at the mercy of someone much larger than they are. I think they are more honest than grown-ups and in more need of strong stories.

Byron brought her complaint to the school district administration, which formed another committee to hold public hearings.

Chairing the committee was Wendy Graves, president-elect of the Minnesota PTA, who asked members to read at least four of the nine books proposed for removal. Graves says that one *Goosebumps* she had read with her daughter was frightening, but its ending was so far-fetched that it seemed unlikely to scare anyone. As elsewhere, *Goosebumps* was very popular in the very school district where the book banning had been requested. The Hennepin County library system's 93 copies of *Welcome to Dead House* had been checked out 5,546 times, an average of about 60 times each, a high rate compared with other books. Ironically, part of the district in question, Anoka, calls itself the "Halloween Capital of the World."

One speaker at the hearings was Cortney Jones, then a ten-year-old fourth grader at Eisenhower Elementary. Jones, who owned about thirty of the *Goosebumps* books, said she learned "that some issues can turn really big even if they sound small. And I learned that we should decide what kinds of books to read." Another *Goosebumps* fancier, Ryan Fischer, a ten-year-old fifth grader at the same school, agreed: "I think that kids should get to choose what books they want to read and what books they don't want to read. If it is too scary for them, don't get it."[97]

During the hearings, only a handful of parents asked that Stine's books be removed. The parents, teachers, and administrators on the committee then voted unanimously that the nine books be kept on the shelves and recommended to the school superintendent that all titles in the series be retained in the district. This decision was based on several factors, among them the fact that the district's school libraries are public. Graves also pointed out that *Goosebumps* books "build fluency in reading by using simple vocabulary, repetitive plots and imaginative content; the books are appropriate for the student age group, allowing children to master fears, whether of monsters under the bed or of being alone, [and] the committee believes students have the right to choose their own reading materials from the library. The responsibility for good decision-making should rest with individual children and their parents." Byron was "very disappointed." "I've lost a lot of faith in the public schools," she says. "Our standards are going way down."[98]

So Successful It's Scary

A children's librarian who criticized the writing, characterization, and plots in *Goosebumps* took the long view, saying, "The only redeeming feature is that this too shall pass. I hope Stine can make enough to retire soon and stop churning them out."[99]

Well, R. L. Stine has already made more than enough money to retire—more than he knows what to do with and indeed more than he says he has the time to spend. It is most unlikely, however, that the author will stop producing books anytime soon.

Claiming that no one is more surprised by his success than he, Stine declared in 1995: "It's hard to believe any of this. . . . The kind of success I've had you can't fantasize about. It's like winning the lottery—except when you win the lottery, you retire." Retirement, however, is apparently not in Stine's plans. He continued, "The kids are afraid that I'm going to quit writing *Goosebumps*. They ask me, or write me letters saying that they've heard I'm going to stop writing *Goosebumps* because of the TV show. I try to tell them that I'll never stop. I enjoy it too much."[100] And a year later, Stine commented on his madcap pace to another writer: "It *is* a lot of work, but the kids' love for these books is so exhilarating that it keeps me going. . . . I hope we can last 10 more years. I think we can."[101]

Apparently Stine's feelings have not changed. By January 1998, he had contracted to continue his series for at least three more years. In addition, the Parachute organization and HarperCollins Children's Books announced that a book of "ten of the most terrifying, original stories R. L. Stine has ever written" would be published in September 1999 under the title *Nightmare Hour*. The announcement claimed the book, aimed at children eight years old and up, would be "the first-ever children's trade hardcover book" by Stine and "the perfect scary treat for kids."[102]

Again Stine reacts to great success by calling himself lucky, telling an interviewer: "I never could have imagined that *Goosebumps* would be so popular. You dream about selling a million books, but no one ever expects 200 million."[103]

Not only in number of books sold has Stine exceeded his aspirations:

> I've achieved everything I've ever wanted to do. More. All I ever wanted in life was to have my own national humor magazine and I had that when I was 28. Everything else has been extra. You can't plan for success like this. It's like winning the lottery.[104]

He donates some of his huge earnings to charity, as he did with a portion of the million-dollar advance he received for his adult book. Among the beneficiaries is an educational program for inner-city youth.

Same Jovial Bob

How has success changed Stine's life? He always replies that he's working harder than he thought he could, and adds that because he and his family do not have lavish tastes, his wealth is essentially wasted on him.

Income from the books and other projects has enabled the Stines to move from the three-bedroom, one-bathroom apartment they rented for twenty-five years on New York City's Upper West Side to a larger one three blocks away. And it has enabled him to indulge one passion: buying first editions of books by his favorite author, the British humorist P. G. Wodehouse, whose first editions fill an entire bookshelf in Stine's apartment. "This will wreck my horror reputation," he jokes. "The thing about Wodehouse is that he lived to be 93, he wrote 93 novels and all of them are exactly the same. I really admire that."[105]

Among other authors he favors is Edgar Allan Poe, the nineteenth-century American master of suspense. Stine's reading tastes are varied; he enjoys humor and novels, including mysteries, especially those by Agatha Christie, which "have wonderful, tricky plots." Another favorite author is children's writer/illustrator Chris Van Allsburg—"wonderfully talented. Very original. Always surprising. I buy all of his books."[106]

Stine hopes that young people will read books of all kinds, too. To young aspiring writers, he advises, "Read, read, read.

Stine's success in the horror genre has enabled him to buy first editions of books by his favorite author, P.G. Wodehouse (pictured).

Read all kinds of books. That way you pick up different styles and learn different ways to say things." Stine tells them not to be in a hurry to submit their stories for publication, pointing out that, "No one really wants to publish work by kids. Just keep writing—and mainly reading and reading." [107]

In Jean Feiwel's view, Stine "has worked long and hard in the children's publishing arena (and) has an appreciation and respect for children, knows their fears, and knows what makes them laugh." [108] The Scholastic publisher does not think it likely that another author will replace Stine as king of the genre.

Yet, as long ago as 1995, Stine acknowledged that "Kids move on. In ten years, they won't be buying these books anymore. They'll be into something else. I think I'll be doing some other things, too." [109] Nevertheless, while observing that everything has its cycle and conceding that his pace may ease when the tremendous wave of popularity recedes, he pictures himself still writing books, but not as often. Says Stine: "Right now I just can't believe this is happening to me. . . . I am having too much fun to stop." [110]

Notes

Chapter 1: Just a Normal, Scary Childhood

1. R. L. Stine, as told to Joe Arthur, *It Came from Ohio! My Life as a Writer.* New York: Parachute Press, Scholastic, 1997, pp. 42–43.
2. Stine, *It Came from Ohio!* p. 9.
3. Quoted in Holly L. Pupino, "A Rash of Goosebumps," *Ohio State Alumni Magazine,* December 1996, p. 17.
4. Stine, *It Came from Ohio!* pp. 33–34.
5. Stine, *It Came from Ohio!* p. 12.
6. Quoted in Pupino, "A Rash of Goosebumps," p. 17.
7. Quoted in Pupino, "A Rash of Goosebumps," p. 17.
8. Quoted in Ross Raihala, "Meet R. L. Stine," *The Forum* (Fargo, ND), n.d.
9. R. L. Stine, America Online (AOL) chat, October 31, 1994.
10. Quoted in Vivian Rose, Hangin' Out with Vivian Rose, "R. L. Stine Giving You Goosebumps," KidsLife, *Tampa Tribune,* September 1, 1997.
11. Quoted in Shawn Sell, "Stine Gives Kids Goosebumps with Frightening Speed," *USA Today,* October 31, 1996.
12. Quoted in James Kaplan, "Scare Tactics," *TV Guide,* October 26–November 1, 1996.
13. Quoted in Ula Ilnytzky, "Meet R. L. Stine, Author of Popular 'Goosebumps,'" *Grand Rapids Press,* December 27, 1995.

Chapter 2: Eloquent Insanity

14. Quoted in Fred Kaplan, "R. L. Stine Takes a Stab at Scaring Adults," *Boston Globe,* December 15, 1995.
15. Stine, *It Came from Ohio!* p. 53.
16. Stine, *It Came from Ohio!* p. 62.

17. Stine, *It Came from Ohio!* pp. 59–60.

Chapter 3: Bologna Sandwiches, Soda Caps, and Bananas

18. Stine, *It Came from Ohio!* pp. 65–66.
19. Stine, *It Came from Ohio!* p. 74.
20. Stine, *It Came from Ohio!* p. 84.
21. Quoted in Ilnytzky, "Meet R. L. Stine, Author of Popular 'Goosebumps.'"
22. Quoted in Fred Kaplan, "Kids' Author Out to Give Grown-Ups Goosebumps," *Detroit News,* December 15, 1995.
23. Quoted in Murray Dubin, "The Stephen King of Preteen Readers," *Philadelphia Inquirer,* May 12, 1996.
24. Quoted in Andrew Billen, "Ghost Writer's Phenomenal Success," *Eagle-Tribune* (Lawrence, MA), October 24, 1996.
25. Quoted in Joyce M. Rosenberg, "Monster Hits," *Tri-City Herald* (Kennewick, WA), October 27, 1996.
26. Quoted in Fred Kaplan, "Kids' Author Out to Give Grown-Ups Goosebumps."
27. Quoted in Dubin, "The Stephen King of Preteen Readers."
28. Quoted in Raihala, "Meet R. L. Stine."
29. Quoted in Sell, "Stine Gives Kids Goosebumps with Frightening Speed."

Chapter 4: R. L.'s M.O.: The Method to Stine's Madness

30. Quoted in Billen, "Ghost Writer's Phenomenal Success."
31. John Lucas, "A New Kiddie Craze: Books!" *Commercial Appeal* (Memphis), n.d.
32. Quoted in Pupino, "A Rash of Goosebumps," p. 17.
33. Quoted in Raihala, "Meet R. L. Stine."
34. Quoted in Dubin, "The Stephen King of Preteen Readers."
35. Quoted in Pupino, "A Rash of Goosebumps," p. 17.
36. Quoted in Fred Kaplan, "Kids' Author Out to Give Grown-Ups Goosebumps."
37. Quoted in Paul Lomartire, "Goosebumps' to Make TV Debut," *Observer Reporter* (Washington, PA), September 3, 1995.
38. Quoted in Ilnytzky, "Meet R. L. Stine, Author of Popular 'Goosebumps.'"
39. Quoted in Pupino, "A Rash of Goosebumps," p. 18.

40. Quoted in "What's Hot," *Denver Post*, July 4, 1995.
41. Quoted in Rose, "R. L. Stine Giving You Goosebumps."
42. Quoted in Dubin, "The Stephen King of Preteen Readers."
43. Quoted in Rose Kennedy, "The Man Who Laughs at Horror," *Disney Adventures*, February 1998.
44. Quoted in Sell, "Stine Gives Kids Goosebumps with Frightening Speed."
45. Tom Collins, "Goosebumps," *News Tribune* (LaSalle, IL), November 29, 1996.
46. Quoted in Harvey Solomon, "Kids Raise 'Goosebumps' to New Heights," *Family Viewing*, September 29–October 5, 1996.
47. Quoted in Raihala, "Meet R. L. Stine."
48. Quoted in Dan Brekke, "Kids Get Their Sought-After 'Goosebumps' on Fox," *San Francisco Examiner*, November 2, 1995.
49. Quoted in Dubin, "The Stephen King of Preteen Readers."
50. James Kaplan, "Scare Tactics."
51. Quoted in "Scary Show for Children Arrives," *Rutherford Courier* (Smyrna, TN), October 26, 1995.
52. Quoted in Denise Gellene, "Series of 'Goosebumps' Books Is a Monster Hit with Children," *San Mateo County Times*, November 29, 1996.
53. Rose, "R. L. Stine Giving You Goosebumps."
54. Quoted in Dubin, "The Stephen King of Preteen Readers."
55. Quoted in Fred Kaplan, "Kids' Author Out to Give Grown-ups Goosebumps."
56. Stine, America Online (AOL) chat.
57. Quoted in Lomartire, "'Goosebumps' to Make TV Debut."

Chapter 5: Popularity: "No One Comes Close"

58. Quoted in Lomartire, "'Goosebumps' to Make TV Debut."
59. Quoted in Mary B. W. Tabor, "Kids' Author Takes Adult Turn," *Cleveland Plain Dealer*, September 13, 1995.
60. Quoted in Fred Kaplan, "Kids' Author Out to Give Grown-ups Goosebumps."
61. Quoted in Fred Kaplan, "Kids' Author Out to Give Grown-ups Goosebumps."
62. Quoted in Tabor, "Kids' Author Takes Adult Turn."
63. Quoted in Fred Kaplan, "Kids' Author Out to Give Grown-

ups Goosebumps."

64. Quoted in Tabor, "Kids' Author Takes Adult Turn."

65. Quoted in Andrew Billen, "How Author R. L. Stine's Career Rose from the Dead," *Minneapolis Star-Tribune*, October 31, 1996.

66. Quoted in Kelly Milner Halls, "It's Getting Bumpier!" *Atlanta Journal*, January 12, 1998.

67. Quoted in Lisa L. Brownlee, "'Goosebumps' Deal Is in the (Doritos) Bag," *Wall Street Journal* (eastern edition), July 10, 1996.

68. Quoted in *St. Petersburg Times*, "'Goosebumps' Promotion Spooks Junk-Food Foes," July 11, 1996.

69. Quoted in Brownlee, "'Goosebumps' Deal Is in the (Doritos) Bag."

70. Quoted in Rosenberg, "Monster Hits."

71. Stine, *It Came from Ohio!* p. 122.

72. Quoted in Laura Lippman, "Giving Them Goosebumps," *Roanoke Times*, March 28, 1996.

73. Quoted in Mark Lorando, "Things That Go 'Bumps' in the Night," *Times-Picayune* (New Orleans), October 22, 1995.

74. Quoted in Michael Mallory, "SCARE FARE: 'Lite Horror' Staple of Young Audience," *Variety*, December 9–15, 1996.

75. James Kaplan, "Scare Tactics."

76. Susan Young, "Fans Can Get Strong Dose of 'Goosebumps' in Prime Time," *Oakland Tribune*, October 27, 1995.

77. Quoted in Susy Schultz, "Goodbye, Goosebumps? No Way! New and Better Chills in Store," *Chicago Sunday Sun-Times*, December 21, 1997.

78. Quoted in Rose, "R. L. Stine, Giving You Goosebumps."

Chapter 6: Mild-Mannered Center of a Storm

79. Quoted in David Wilkison, "Cold Chills Are Hot with Kids," *Philadelphia Daily News*, October 28, 1996.

80. Quoted in Don O'Briant, "Giving Adults Goosebumps," *Atlanta Journal*, September 18, 1995.

81. Quoted in Raihala, "Meet R. L. Stine."

82. Quoted in Walt Belcher, "Things That Go 'Bump' on the Tube," *Tampa Tribune*, n.d.

83. Quoted in Raihala, "Meet R. L. Stine."

84. Quoted in Gellene, "Series of 'Goosebumps' Books Is a Monster Hit with Children."

85. Quoted in Lucas, "A New Kiddie Craze: Books!"

86. Quoted in Mary Jane Smetanka, "Call for Banning Books Has Series on Hot Seat," *Minneapolis Star-Tribune,* January 4, 1997.

87. Quoted in Billie Jo Shepherd, "Goosebump Epidemic Hits East County Hard," *Daily Californian* (El Cajon), October 27, 1996.

88. Quoted in John Grossberg, "Getting Under Their Skin," *Brentwood-Westwood Press* (Brentwood, CA), October 19, 1995.

89. Quoted in Theresa Walker, "Goosebumps Books for Kids Are So Successful, It's Scary," *Orange County Register* (Santa Ana, CA), June 21, 1996.

90. Quoted in Pupino, "A Rash of Goosebumps," p. 18.

91. Quoted in Wilkison, "Cold Chills Are Hot with Kids."

92. Quoted in *Mediakids,* "Why Kids Are Under R. L. Stine's Spell," October 1996.

93. Quoted in Wilkison, "Cold Chills Are Hot with Kids."

94. Katherine Kersten, "These Books Induce Fear While Driving Out Pity," *Minneapolis Star-Tribune,* January 29, 1997.

95. Bob Minzesheimer, "The Leaders of the Banned," *USA Today,* September 18, 1997.

96. Quoted in Theresa Monsour, "Anoka-Hennepin Schools Consider Book Ban," *St. Paul Pioneer Press,* January 3, 1997.

97. Quoted in Theresa Monsour, "Goosebumps Books Will Remain on Shelves," *St. Paul Pioneer Press,* February 5, 1997.

98. Quoted in Monsour, "Goosebumps Books Will Remain on Shelves."

99. Quoted in Jennifer Strobel, "Giving Kids Goosebumps," *Free Lance-Star* (Fredericksburg, VA), October 30, 1995.

100. Quoted in John Kiesewetter, "Kids' Favorite 'Goosebumps' Stories Set for TV Debut," *Progress Tribune* (Scottsdale, AZ), October 27, 1995.

101. Quoted in Sell, "Stine Gives Kids Goosebumps with Frightening Speed."

102. Parachute/HarperCollins press release, January 1998.

103. Quoted in Kim Haub, "Got Goosebumps?" My Word,

Seattle Times, December 13, 1997.

104. Quoted in Lippman, "Giving Them 'Goosebumps.'"
105. Quoted in Fred Kaplan, "Kids' Author Out to Give Grown-Ups Goosebumps."
106. Stine, America Online (AOL) chat.
107. Stine, America Online (AOL) chat.
108. Quoted in Pupino, "A Rash of Goosebumps," p. 18.
109. Quoted in Tabor, "Kids' Author Takes Adult Turn."
110. Quoted in Pupino, "A Rash of Goosebumps," p. 18.

Important Dates in the Life of R. L. Stine

1943

Robert Lawrence (R. L.) Stine is born in Columbus, Ohio, on October 8.

1961

Enters Ohio State University, where, as "Jovial Bob," he becomes editor of *Sundial,* a humor magazine that satirizes all aspects of campus life.

1964

Although seniors are not eligible, in his senior year runs for presidency of student senate, pledging to "do nothing."

1965

Graduates from Ohio State University. Takes job as teacher and lets his history class students read anything they want, including comic books, on Fridays.

1966

Moves to New York City. Secures writing jobs, one for a soft drink industry trade magazine, then for a short-lived group of magazines for which he is assigned to write made-up celebrity interviews.

1968

Joins Scholastic, Inc., children's publisher, as a staff writer on the magazine *Junior Scholastic,* then writes for and edits company publications.

1969

Marries Jane Waldhorn (his future editor).

1975

Realizing a lifelong dream, Stine is assigned to create and edit his own humor magazine, *Bananas*, for Scholastic.

1978

E. P. Dutton releases *How to Be Funny*, Stine's first published children's book.

1980

Bob and Jane's only child, Matthew Daniel Stine, is born.

1984

With demise of *Bananas*, Bob is let go by Scholastic. Undertakes a variety of freelance writing work, from bubblegum cards to computer magazines, coloring books, G.I. Joe adventure novels, and James Bond and Indiana Jones books.

1986

Scholastic publishes Stine's first horror novel, *Blind Date*.

1989

Stine's *Fear Street* series is launched with publication of *The New Girl* by Pocket Books.

1992

Goosebumps debuts with *Welcome to Dead House*.

1995

Superstitious, a Stine horror novel for adults, is published by Warner Books. *Goosebumps* debuts on television, with an hour-long Halloween special, "The Haunted Mask," followed by a weekly series of half-hour episodes based on the books. Stine serves as consultant.

1997

Golden Books acquires rights to sixty-five new *Fear Street* titles, under a joint imprint of Parachute and Golden. *Goosebumps* inspires an attraction at Disney-MGM Studios in Orlando, Florida: the *Goosebumps* HorrorLand Fright Show and Fun House.

1998

Goosebumps Series 2000 makes its debut. Parachute Publishing and HarperCollins Children's Books announce scheduled September 1999 publication of *Nightmare Hour*, a hardcover trade book for children, comprising ten terrifying original Stine stories.

For Further Reading

Patrick Jones, *What's So Scary About R. L. Stine?* Lanham, MD: Scarecrow Studies in Young Adult Literature, Scarecrow Press, 1998. Jones, a Houston young adult librarian, traces Stine's literary career, analyzes his plotting, characterization, and style, and evaluates his standing among respected young adult authors.

James Kaplan, "Scare Tactics," *TV Guide*, October 26–November 1, 1996.

Holly L. Pupino, "A Rash of Goosebumps," *Ohio State Alumni Magazine*, December 1996.

Shawn Sell, "Stine Gives Kids Goosebumps with Frightening Speed," *USA Today*, October 31, 1996.

Jill C. Wheeler, *R. L. Stine (The Young at Heart)*. Edina, MN: ABDO, 1996. A biography of the prolific author, whose humor balances the intense scare factor of his horror novels.

Works Consulted

Books

R. L. Stine, as told to Joe Arthur, *It Came from Ohio! My Life as a Writer*. New York: Parachute Press, Scholastic, 1997.

Periodicals

Walt Belcher, "Things That Go 'Bump' on the Tube," *Tampa Tribune*, n.d.

Andrew Billen, "Ghost Writer's Phenomenal Success," *Eagle-Tribune* (Lawrence, MA), October 24, 1966.

———, "How Author R. L. Stine's Career Rose from the Dead," *Minneapolis Star-Tribune*, October 31, 1996.

Dan Brekke, "Kids Get Their Sought-After 'Goosebumps' on Fox," *San Francisco Examiner*, November 2, 1995.

Lisa L. Brownlee, "'Goosebumps' Deal Is in the (Doritos) Bag," *Wall Street Journal* (eastern edition), July 10, 1996.

Tom Collins, "Goosebumps," *News Tribune* (LaSalle, IL), November 29, 1996.

Denver Post, "What's Hot," July 4, 1995.

Murray Dubin, "R. L. Stine Give Kids 'Goosebumps,'" *Express* (Easton, PA), June 9, 1996.

———, "The Stephen King of Preteen Readers," *Philadelphia Inquirer*, May 12, 1966.

William Flannery, "'Goosebumps' Publisher Goes Thump on Wall Street," *St. Louis Post-Dispatch*, February 22, 1997.

Denise Gellene, "Series of 'Goosebumps' Books Is a Monster Hit with Children," *San Mateo County Times*, November 29, 1996.

John Grossberg, "Getting Under Their Skin," *Brentwood-Westwood Press* (Brentwood, CA), October 19, 1995.

Kelly Milner Halls, "It's Getting Bumpier!" *Atlanta Journal,* January 12, 1998.

Kim Haub, "Got Goosebumps?" My Word, *Seattle Times,* December 13, 1997.

Paul Higbie, "In the Lair of the Horrormeister, *Hartford Courant,* November 2, 1995.

Ula Ilnytzky, "Meet R. L. Stine, Author of Popular 'Goosebumps,'" *Grand Rapids Press,* December 27, 1995.

Fred Kaplan, "Kids' Author Out to Give Grown-Ups Goosebumps," *Detroit News,* December 15, 1995.

———, "R. L. Stine Takes a Stab at Scaring Adults," *Boston Globe,* December 15, 1995.

Rose Kennedy, "The Man Who Laughs at Horror," *Disney Adventures,* February 1998.

Katherine Kersten, "These Books Induce Fear While Driving Out Pity," *Minneapolis Star-Tribune,* January 29, 1997.

John Kiesewetter, "Kids' Favorite 'Goosebumps' Stories Set for TV Debut," *Progress Tribune* (Scottsdale, AZ), October 27, 1995.

Laura Lippman, "Giving Them Goosebumps," *Roanoke Times,* March 28, 1996.

Paul Lomartire, "'Goosebumps' to Make TV Debut," *Observer Reporter* (Washington, PA), September 3, 1995.

Mark Lorando, "Things That Go 'Bumps' in the Night," *Times-Picayune* (New Orleans), October 22, 1995.

John Lucas, "A New Kiddie Craze: Books!" *Commercial Appeal* (Memphis), n.d.

Makio, Ohio State University Yearbook, 1963.

Makio, Ohio State University Yearbook, 1964.

Makio, Ohio State University Yearbook, 1965.

Michael Mallory, "SCARE FARE: 'Lite Horror' Staple of Young Audience," *Variety,* December 9–15, 1996.

Mediakids, "Why Kids Are Under R. L. Stine's Spell," October 1996.

Bob Minzesheimer, "The Leaders of the Banned," *USA Today,* September 18, 1997.

Theresa Monsour, "Anoka-Hennepin Schools Consider Book Ban," *St. Paul Pioneer Press,* January 3, 1997.

———, "Goosebumps Books Will Remain on Shelves," *St. Paul Pioneer Press,* February 5, 1997.

New York Times, Book Country advertisement, September 23, 1997.

Don O'Briant, "Giving Adults Goosebumps," *Atlanta Journal,* September 18, 1995.

Kate O'Hare, "R. L. Stine Gives Kids 'Goosebumps,'" *Baltimore Sun,* June 16, 1996.

Ross Raihala, "Meet R. L. Stine," *The Forum* (Fargo, ND), n.d.

Vivian Rose, Hangin' Out with Vivian Rose, "R. L. Stine Giving You Goosebumps," KidsLife, *Tampa Tribune,* September 1, 1997.

Joyce M. Rosenberg, "Goosebumps," *San Diego Union-Tribune,* October 27, 1996.

———, "Monster Hits," *Tri-City Herald* (Kennewick, WA), October 27, 1996.

Rutherford Courier (Smyrna, TN), "Scary Show for Children Arrives," October 26, 1995.

Susy Schultz, "Goodbye, Goosebumps? No Way! New and Better Chills in Store," *Chicago Sunday Sun-Times,* December 21, 1997.

Billie Jo Shepherd, "Goosebumps Epidemic Hits East County Hard," *Daily Californian* (El Cajon), October 27, 1996.

Mary Jane Smetanka, "Call for Banning Books Has Series on Hot Seat," *Minneapolis Star-Tribune,* January 4, 1997.

Harvey Solomon, "Kids Raise 'Goosebumps' to New Heights," *Family Viewing,* September 29–October 5, 1996.

St. Petersburg Times, "'Goosebumps' Promotion Spooks Junk-Food Foes," July 11, 1996.

Jennifer Strobel, "Giving Kids Goosebumps," *Free Lance-Star* (Fredericksburg, VA), October 30, 1995.

Mary B. W. Tabor, "Kids' Author Takes Adult Turn," *Cleveland Plain Dealer*, September 13, 1995.

Theresa Walker, "Goosebumps Books for Kids Are So Successful, It's Scary," *Orange County Register* (Santa Ana, CA), June 21, 1996.

David Wilkison, "Children Zombie-Like in Devotion," *Cleveland Plain Dealer,* November 28, 1996.

————, "Cold Chills Are Hot with Kids," *Philadelphia Daily News*, October 28, 1996.

Susan Young, "Fans Can Get Strong Dose of 'Goosebumps' in Prime Time," *Oakland Tribune*, October 27, 1995.

Internet

R. L. Stine, America Online (AOL) chat, October 31, 1994.

Index

Picture Credits

Cover photo: AP Photo
© Frank Capri/SAGA/Archive Photos, 14, 26, 71 (bottom)
Corbis-Bettmann, 9, 15, 53
© Fox Broadcasting Company/Photofest, 47, 60
Darlene Hammond/Archive Photos, 54
© Sandra Johnson/SAGA/Archive Photos, 63
Museum of the City of New York/Archive Photos, 71 (top)
The Ohio State University Archives, 22, 23, 25, 27
Photofest, 13, 31, 43, 59, 62, 69
Seth Poppel Yearbook Archives, 20, 21
Scholastic, Inc., 37
© F. Veronsky/Sygma, 7, 38, 42

About the Author

Joel H. Cohen is the author of more than thirty books, most of them for young readers, and most with or about prominent athletes and entertainers. Among them are Hank Aaron, Bill Cosby, Jim Palmer, Lucille Ball, Tom Seaver, Johnny Unitas, Kareem Abdul-Jabbar, and several champion female gymnasts. His most recent book is a biography about illustrator Norman Rockwell. Cohen's articles and essays have appeared in various magazines and newspapers, including *TV Guide, Parents, Sports Illustrated for Kids, Ingenue,* the *New York Times,* the *Chicago Tribune,* and the *Staten Island Advance.* He and his wife live in Staten Island, New York, and have four grown children.